RACHEL CARSON

RACHEL CARSON

MARTY JEZER

CHELSEA HOUSE PUBLISHERS

PHILADELPHIA

Chelsea House Publishers

EDITOR-IN-CHIEF: Nancy Toff
EXECUTIVE EDITOR: Remmel T. Nunn
MANAGING EDITOR: Karyn Gullen Browne
COPY CHIEF: Juliann Barbato
PICTURE EDITOR: Adrian G. Allen
ART DIRECTOR: Giannella Garrett
MANUFACTURING MANAGER: Gerald Levine

American Women of Achievement
SENIOR EDITOR: Constance Jones

Staff for RACHEL CARSON
ASSISTANT EDITOR: Maria Behan
COPY EDITOR: Karen Hammonds
DEPUTY COPY CHIEF: Ellen Scordato
EDITORIAL ASSISTANT: Theodore Keyes
PICTURE RESEARCHER: Susan Biederman
DESIGN: Design Oasis
ASSISTANT DESIGNER: Donna Sinisgalli
PRODUCTION COORDINATOR: Joseph Romano
COVER ILLUSTRATOR: © Michael Garland

9

Library of Congress Cataloging-in-Publication Data

Jezer, Marty. Rachel Carson

(American women of achievement)
Bibliography: p.
Summary: A biography of the marine biologist and author whose
writings stressed the interrelation of all living things and the dependence of human welfare on natural processes.
[1. Carson, Rachel, 1907–1964—Juvenile literature.   2. Women
conservationists—United States—Biography—Juvenile literature.
3. Conservationists—United States—Biography—Juvenile
literature.   1. Carson, Rachel, 1907–1964.   2. Conservationists.
3. Biologists]   I. Title.   II. Series

Library of Congress Cataloging-in-Publication Data

QH31.C33J48   1988   574′.092′4 [B] [92]   87-27821

ISBN 1-55546-646-X
     0-7910-0413-9 (pbk.)

CONTENTS

WOMEN of ACHIEVEMENT

Abigail Adams
WOMEN'S RIGHTS ADVOCATE

Jane Addams
SOCIAL WORKER

Madeleine Albright
STATESWOMAN

Louisa May Alcott
AUTHOR

Marian Anderson
SINGER

Susan B. Anthony
WOMAN SUFFRAGIST

Ethel Barrymore
ACTRESS

Clara Barton
AMERICAN RED CROSS FOUNDER

Elizabeth Blackwell
PHYSICIAN

Pearl Buck
AUTHOR

Margaret Bourke-White
PHOTOGRAPHER

Rachel Carson
BIOLOGIST AND AUTHOR

Mary Cassatt
ARTIST

Hillary Rodham Clinton
FIRST LADY/ATTORNEY

Diana, Princess of Wales
HUMANITARIAN

Emily Dickinson
POET

Isadora Duncan
DANCER

Amelia Earhart
AVIATOR

Betty Friedan
FEMINIST

Althea Gibson
TENNIS CHAMPION

Helen Hayes
ACTRESS

Katharine Hepburn
ACTRESS

Anne Hutchinson
RELIGIOUS LEADER

Mahalia Jackson
GOSPEL SINGER

Helen Keller
HUMANITARIAN

Jeane Kirkpatrick
DIPLOMAT

Barbara McClintock
BIOLOGIST

Margaret Mead
ANTHROPOLOGIST

Edna St. Vincent Millay
POET

Agnes de Mille
CHOREOGRAPHER

Julia Morgan
ARCHITECT

Grandma Moses
PAINTER

Georgia O'Keeffe
PAINTER

Sandra Day O'Connor
SUPREME COURT JUSTICE

Rosie O'Donnell
ENTERTAINER/COMEDIENNE

Eleanor Roosevelt
DIPLOMAT AND HUMANITARIAN

Wilma Rudolph
CHAMPION ATHLETE

Gloria Steinem
FEMINIST

Harriet Beecher Stowe
AUTHOR AND ABOLITIONIST

Elizabeth Taylor
ACTRESS/ACTIVIST

Barbara Walters
JOURNALIST

Edith Wharton
AUTHOR

Phyllis Wheatley
POET

Babe Didrikson Zaharias
CHAMPION ATHLETE

"Remember the Ladies"

MATINA S. HORNER

Remember the Ladies." That is what Abigail Adams wrote to her husband John, then a delegate to the Continental Congress, as the Founding Fathers met in Philadelphia to form a new nation in March of 1776. "Be more generous and favorable to them than your ancestors. Do not put such unlimited power in the hands of the Husbands. If particular care and attention is not paid to the Ladies," Abigail Adams warned, "we are determined to foment a Rebellion, and will not hold ourselves bound by any Laws in which we have no voice, or Representation."

The words of Abigail Adams, one of the earliest American advocates of women's rights, were prophetic. Because when we have not "remembered the ladies," they have, by their words and deeds, reminded us so forcefully of the omission that we cannot fail to remember them. For the history of American women is as interesting and varied as the history of our nation as a whole. American women have played an integral part in founding, settling, and building our country. Some we remember as remarkable women who—against great odds—achieved distinction in the public arena: Anne Hutchinson, who in the 17th century became a charismatic religious leader; Phillis Wheatley, an 18th-century black slave who became a poet; Susan B. Anthony, whose name is synonymous with the 19th-century women's rights movement, and who led the struggle to enfranchise women; and, in our own century, Amelia Earhart, the first woman to cross the Atlantic Ocean by air.

These extraordinary women certainly merit our admiration, but other women, "common women," many of them all but forgotten, should also be recognized for their contributions to American thought and culture. Women have been community builders; they have founded schools and formed voluntary associations to help those in need; they have assumed the major responsibility for rearing children, passing on from one generation to the next the values that keep a culture alive. These and innumerable other contributions, once ignored, are now being recognized by scholars, students, and the public. It is exciting and gratifying to realize that a part of our history that was hardly acknowledged a few generations ago is now being studied and brought to light.

In recent decades, the field of women's history has grown from obscurity to a politically controversial splinter movement to academic respectability, in many cases mainstreamed into such traditional disciplines as history, economics, and psychology. Scholars of women, both female and male, have organized research centers at such prestigious institutions as Wellesley College, Stanford University, and the University of California. Other notable centers for women's studies are the Center for the American Woman and Politics at the Eagleton Institute of Politics at Rutgers University; the Henry A. Murray Research Center for the Study of Lives, at Radcliffe College; and the Women's Research and Education Institute, the research arm of the Congressional Caucus on Women's Issues. Other scholars and public figures have established archives and libraries, such as the Schlesinger Library on the History of Women in America, at Radcliffe College, and the Sophia Smith Collection, at Smith College, to collect and preserve the written and tangible legacies of women.

From the initial donation of the Women's Rights Collection in 1943, the Schlesinger Library grew to encompass vast collections documenting the manifold accomplishments of American women. Simultaneously, the women's movement in general and the academic discipline of women's studies in particular also began with a narrow definition and gradually expanded their mandate. Early causes such as woman suffrage and social reform, abolition and organized labor were joined by newer concerns such as the history of women in business and the professions and in politics and government; the study of the family; and social issues such as health policy and education.

Women, as historian Arthur M. Schlesinger, jr., once pointed out, "have constituted the most spectacular casualty of traditional history. They have made up at least half the human race, but you could never tell that by looking at the books historians write." The new breed of historians is remedying that omission. They have written books about immigrant women and about working-class women who struggled for survival in cities and about black women who met the challenges of life in rural areas. They are telling the stories of women who, despite the barriers of tradition and economics, became lawyers and doctors and public figures.

The women's studies movement has also led scholars to question traditional interpretations of their respective disciplines. For example, the study of war has traditionally been an exercise in military and political analysis, an examination of strategies planned and executed by men. But scholars of women's history have pointed out that wars have also been periods of tremendous change and even opportunity for women, because the very absence of men on the home front enabled them to expand their educational, economic, and professional activities and to assume leadership in their homes.

The early scholars of women's history showed a unique brand of courage in choosing to investigate new subjects and take new approaches to old ones. Often, like their subjects, they endured criticism and even ostracism by their academic colleagues. But their efforts have unquestionably been worthwhile, because with the publication of each new study and book another piece of the historical patchwork is sewn into place, revealing an increasingly comprehensive picture of the role of women in our rich and varied history.

Such books on groups of women are essential, but books that focus on the lives of individuals are equally indispensable. Biographies can be inspirational, offering their readers the example of people with vision who have looked outside themselves for their goals and have often struggled against great obstacles to achieve them. Marian Anderson, for instance, had to overcome racial bigotry in order to perfect her art and perform as a concert singer. Isadora Duncan defied the rules of classical dance to find true artistic freedom. Jane Addams had to break down society's notions of the proper role for women in order to create new social institutions, notably the settlement house. All of these women had to come to terms both with themselves and with the world in which they lived. Only then could they move ahead as pioneers in their chosen callings.

Biography can inspire not only by adulation but also by realism. It helps us to see not only the qualities in others that we hope to emulate, but also, perhaps, the weaknesses that made them "human." By helping us identify with the subject on a more personal level they help us to feel that we, too, can achieve such goals. We read about Eleanor Roosevelt, for instance, who occupied a unique and seemingly enviable position as the wife of the president. Yet we can sympathize with her inner dilemma: an inherently shy woman, she had to force herself to live a most public life in order to use her position to benefit others. We may not be able to imagine ourselves having the immense poetic talent of Emily Dickinson, but from her story we can understand the challenges faced by a creative woman who was expected to fulfill many family responsibilities. And though few of us will ever reach the level of athletic accomplishment displayed by Wilma Rudolph or Babe Zaharias, we can still appreciate their spirit, their overwhelming will to excel.

A biography is a multifaceted lens. It is first of all a magnification, the intimate examination of one particular life. But at the same time, it is a wide-angle lens, informing us about the world in which the subject lived. We come away from reading about one life knowing more about the social, political, and economic fabric of the time. It is for this reason, perhaps, that the great New England essayist Ralph Waldo Emerson wrote, in 1841, "There is properly no history: only biography." And it is also why biography, and particularly women's biography, will continue to fascinate writers and readers alike.

RACHEL CARSON

Appearing on a 1963 television program exploring the implications of her book Silent Spring, *Rachel Carson discusses pesticide use with journalist Eric Sevareid.*

ONE

Contentious Spring

On April 3, 1963, biologist Rachel Carson appeared on a controversial CBS television show. Previously, Carson had been known for her books about the sea, but her most recent work examined a new—and hotly debated—topic. Even before televising the program, the Columbia Broadcasting System had been hit with a barrage of more than 1,000 letters. Many of the letters criticized the very idea of airing the show, called "The Silent Spring of Rachel Carson." As the broadcast date drew near, three of the five original sponsors withdrew their support in order to distance themselves from the dispute. Nonetheless, the program aired as planned, featuring Carson, four representatives of the United States government, and chemist Dr. Robert White-Stevens.

The broadcast spotlighted a debate that had raged since the publication of Carson's explosive book, *Silent Spring*, six months earlier. *Silent Spring* documented the horrifying impact of newly developed chemical pesticides on the natural environment. Carson's careful research had yielded persuasive evidence that the uncontrolled use of powerful insect-controlling poisons was as potentially dangerous to life on earth as nuclear war. She urged others to do further research, for without it, no one could be certain of the long-term effect these chemicals might have on soil, water, animals, or human beings.

Like Carson's previous best-sellers, *Silent Spring* received great public and critical acclaim, but it also sparked a heated dispute. Supporters of the politically influential pesticide industry opposed Carson. *Time* magazine labeled *Silent Spring* "unfair,

Supreme Court Justice William O. Douglas admired Silent Spring, *which he termed "the most important chronicle of this century for the human race."*

tal changes in the way they treated the planet. Although farmers had always tried to control weeds and crop-eating insects, until recently they had fought pests using methods that did little or no damage to the environment. During World War II, however, a new generation of pesticides, far more toxic than anything that had been used before, came into use. In the 1950s agriculture and forestry experts had routinely encouraged the use of these pesticides on croplands, forests, shade trees, and shrubs. Chemicals were widely used to eradicate crabgrass on lawns, kill insect pests in the home, and control plant growth beside highways and on railroad lines. By 1960 there were some 200 different chemical formulations used in pesticide production. That same year almost 638 million pounds of pesticides flooded into the environment. People had come to rely on these chemicals, but according to the dire warnings in *Silent Spring*, they could no longer do so without seriously harming the environment.

The manufacture of chemical pesticides was a $250 million business with the potential, industry experts believed, for unlimited growth. By attacking pesticide use as dangerous, *Silent Spring* jeopardized the profits of chemical manufacturers. In response, the industry launched a massive counterattack. Unable to undermine Carson's forceful scientific arguments, the heads of several large pesticide com-

one-sided, and hysterically overemphatic." But conservationists, who feared that the environment could be permanently damaged by pollutants, praised Carson's work. To Justice William O. Douglas of the United States Supreme Court, *Silent Spring* was nothing less than "the most important chronicle of this century for the human race."

The questions raised by *Silent Spring* reverberated throughout the country. If Carson was right, people would have to make some fundamen-

A man surveys the arsenal of chemicals used in a typical year on his 78-acre farm. Alarmed by the routine use of pesticides, Carson called for a saner approach to pest control.

panies instead mounted a public relations campaign aimed at destroying Carson's credibility as a scientist and writer. "One obvious way to try to weaken a cause is to discredit the person who champions it," Carson remarked when she heard about their efforts. "So—the masters of invective and insinuation have been busy."

Chemical industry officials tried to convince the public that the author of *Silent Spring* was a sentimental, naive dreamer who did not know what she was talking about. One industry representative characterized Carson as part of a "vociferous, misinformed group of nature-balancing, organic-gardening, bird-loving, unreasonable citizenry that has not been convinced of the important place of agricultural chemicals in our economy."

Disgusted by the shrill tenor of the campaign against *Silent Spring*, Carson tried to stay out of the fray and allow her painstakingly researched book to speak for itself. But when CBS News approached her about its program "The Silent Spring of Rachel Carson," she could not refuse the opportunity to air her views and answer her critics. She decided to allow journalist Eric Sevareid to tape an interview in her Maine home.

Sevareid also interviewed Carson's most relentless opponent, Dr. White-Stevens, assistant director of research for the American Cyanamid Company. For the past several months, White-Stevens had been traveling around the country denouncing *Silent Spring*. Now, eager to win over as many people as possible, he too took full advantage of the opportunity to speak to CBS's massive prime-time audience.

"The major claims of Miss Rachel Carson's book are gross distortions of the actual facts, completely unsupported by scientific evidence," he charged. As he had done before, White-Stevens asserted that if Carson's theories were put into practice, hordes of insects would sweep over the land, devouring crops, destroying forests, and decimating the food supply. Widespread hunger and starvation, he said, would imperil civilization itself. "We would return to the Dark Ages," he announced dramatically, "and the insects and vermin would once again inherit the earth."

Carson was not intimidated by Dr. White-Stevens's ominous pronouncements. She had heard this kind of harsh and exaggerated criticism before. Although the television show's format prevented her from engaging in a face-to-face debate with her opponent, she made statements that she knew would refute his arguments. Where Dr. White-Stevens denied that chemical pesticides had any ill effect on human beings or the natural environment, Carson cited evidence to the contrary. "Can anyone believe it is possible to lay down such a barrage of poisons on the surface of the earth without making it unfit for all life?" she asked the television audience.

Government officials presented their views over the air as well. The federal government, especially the U.S. Department of Agriculture, had previously cooperated with the chemical industry in advocating pesticide use and had argued that chemicals could be assumed safe unless field experience proved otherwise. Now, because of *Silent Spring*, government officials were on the defensive and faced growing political pressure to change their policies. Secretary of Agriculture Orville Freeman conceded as much during his appearance on "The Silent Spring of Rachel Carson." Carson's book, he admitted, had convinced the Kennedy administration to review its position on pesticides. Alarmed by Carson's evidence, state and federal officials were beginning to realize that the dangers she warned of could no longer be ignored.

But the dispute put more at stake than the income of a few corporations or the reputation of the U.S. government. On the most basic level, the controversy centered on philosophies of life, different ways of looking at the relationship between human beings and the natural world. As Paul Brooks, the editor of *Silent Spring*, wrote, "Her opponents must have realized—as was indeed the case—that she was questioning not only the indiscriminate use of poisons but the basic irresponsibil-

Dr. Robert White-Stevens, a chemical company executive, examines pesticide-treated plants. White-Stevens was Silent Spring's *most outspoken opponent.*

Farmers flee a swarm of locusts. Silent Spring's *detractors maintained that the application of Carson's ideas would unleash a devastating onslaught of insects.*

ity of an industrialized, technological society toward the natural world. She refused to accept the premise that damage to nature was the inevitable cost of 'progress.'"

In the opinion of Dr. White-Stevens, Carson had a "backward" view of progress. The forces of nature that governed the lives of animals and plants were no longer important for human survival, he asserted. On the contrary, he said, nature was something for scientists to subdue, manipulate, and conquer. In Dr. White-

Stevens's eyes, the goal of science was not to protect the balance of nature but to improve the conditions of human life.

Carson did not consider this viewpoint enlightened science. Reiterating the ideas expressed in *Silent Spring,* she told the television audience: "We still talk in terms of conquest. We still haven't become mature enough to think of ourselves as only a tiny part of a vast and incredible universe. Man's attitude toward nature is today critically important simply because we have now acquired a fateful power to alter and destroy nature. But man is a part of nature, and his war against nature is inevitably a war against himself."

Carson also outlined her philosophy of ecology during the television interview. She pointed out that "the balance of nature is built of a series of inter-relationships between living things, and between living things and their environment." According to this theory, every plant and every animal—whether tiny microbe or human being—has an essential part to play in the survival of life on earth. "You can't just step in with some brute force and change one thing without changing a good many others," she warned. Yet Carson was not opposed to scientific progress, as her detractors implied. All she demanded was that those who pursued technological advancement did so cautiously, weighing the consequences of their actions on the natural order.

The conflict surrounding the publication of *Silent Spring* had thrust Rachel Carson into the role of environmental crusader. A shy, soft-spoken 55-year-old, she would have preferred to avoid the spotlight. Carson thought of herself as a scientist and writer, not as a public personality or political leader. Her lifelong appetite for solitude grew even stronger after she fell gravely ill with cancer, which sapped her strength and often caused her

Secretary of Agriculture Orville Freeman appeared on "The Silent Spring of Rachel Carson" to discuss the effects of Carson's book on public policy.

An atomic bomb explodes over the Japanese city of Hiroshima in 1945. Carson warned that chemical pesticides were as potentially lethal as nuclear war.

public's response to the show was startling, more than Carson—or anyone—had expected. Letters poured in to CBS and to the country's political leaders commending her efforts and urging the government to take action to protect the environment. Sales of *Silent Spring* skyrocketed. Much to her discomfort, Carson became a celebrity and a household name.

Every once in a while a book profoundly and irrevocably changes the course of human history. *Silent Spring* is certainly such a work. Paul Brooks, Carson's editor, compared it to Darwin's groundbreaking book on evolution, published more than a century earlier. "Perhaps not since the classic controversy over Charles Darwin's *The Origin of Species*," he remarked, "had a single book been more bitterly attacked by those who felt their interests threatened."

When Carson wrote *Silent Spring*, few scientists understood the potential dangers of chemical pesticides, and the principles of ecology were undeveloped. To many Americans of the period, the notion of spending time and effort to keep the atmosphere and water supply clean was almost incomprehensible. The debate surrounding Carson's book made the spring of 1963 politically contentious—and marked the beginning of the modern environmental movement. Once people became concerned about the effects of chemical pesticides on the environ-

great pain. But recognizing the terrible dangers that chemical pesticides posed, she could not allow her opponents to discredit her findings and obstruct further vital research.

CBS's "The Silent Spring of Rachel Carson" allowed Carson to present her case and answer her critics before a nationwide television audience. The ment, they began to examine other forms of pollution: air filled with sulfur, ash, and soot; oceans, lakes, and rivers coated with oil slicks and chemical slime; rain tainted with dangerous acid; food treated with chemical additives; nuclear power plants springing up around the country; and toxic waste dumped in the ocean or stored underground. All these previously accepted facts of life came into question.

These issues are raised regularly today, and science and industry strive to respond to them. But before Rachel Carson's book became a best-seller, few people bothered to think about the environment. Published in 16 countries and translated into almost as many languages, *Silent Spring* was the catalyst that inspired people all over the world to reconsider their place on the planet and take responsibility for the environment.

This 1963 cartoon parodies the impassioned debate occasioned by Silent Spring. *The caption reads, "Just say the blow was inflicted by a blunt instrument."*

Born in 1907, Rachel Carson grew up on a quiet Pennsylvania farm set in the heart of coal and steel country.

TWO

Springdale Oasis

Rachel Louise Carson was born on May 27, 1907, in Springdale, Pennsylvania, a small community nestled in the Allegheny River valley. She spent her childhood on a modest 65-acre homestead set on a hill overlooking a great bend in the river. The Carson farm was an oasis of sorts, a tract of unscarred natural beauty in the midst of a spreading industrial landscape.

This was coal and steel country. Broken rubble drawn up from mine shafts dug deep into the ground lay in great slag heaps that marred the countryside. The valley of the Allegheny, which the Indians had called the "Great River" or "Beautiful River," had been transformed into a polluted transportation corridor for barges and freight trains hauling coal, steel, and other industrial products to and from the blast furnaces of the local steel mills.

Rachel Carson grew up during a period of great industrial expansion in the United States. Pittsburgh, 11 miles Southwest of Springdale, was a booming steel center, and its population was spilling over into neighboring towns. Robert and Maria Carson, Rachel's parents, had purchased their farm in the belief that Springdale would grow as Pittsburgh boomed. Robert Carson planned to divide the farm into small building lots, reaping a profit as he sold them off.

Rachel's father was a businessman—but not a very energetic one. When his plan to sell the land failed, he sold insurance, and when that job did not pay enough he went to work at the local power generating station. Al-

Maria Carson sits for a formal portrait with her children (from left to right) Marian, Rachel, and Robert, Jr.

though he had grown up in urban Pittsburgh, he came from a family that included several farmers, and he wanted to continue the tradition. No matter how he was employed during his adult years, he and his wife continued to work on their farm. But except for a little money they made selling apples from their 10-acre orchard, the farm did not provide the family with any income.

A woman of great personal integrity, Maria Carson had a tremendous influ-

ence on her daughter's life. After her father died when she was 11, Maria had been raised in a household of women in Washington, Pennsylvania. She grew into a confident, self-reliant young woman and became a teacher, largely because it was one of few career opportunities open to middle-class women at the time. But her special love was music. Music, in fact, had brought her and Robert Carson together: They met when he was visiting Washington with a traveling church singing group. The couple married in 1894 and moved to the Springdale farm six years later.

Like their neighbors, the Carsons believed in industrial progress, but they were also strongly attached to rural life. When a coal company offered the family some much-needed money in exchange for the right to extend a mine shaft under the farm, the Carsons refused. A mine shaft deep in the ground would not mar the surface, but keeping the land inviolate was important to Rachel's mother and father. They later suspected that the coal company was digging under the farm without their permission, yet they were powerless to do anything about it because they had no way to prove their charges. Their convictions might not have mattered to the industrialists, but Robert and Maria Carson's views certainly had an impact on their daughter Rachel. They not only imbued her with a respect for the land,

Soil is removed during strip mining. Because of their respect for the land, Rachel's parents refused to allow a coal company to dig under their farm.

Rachel (center) joins her brother and sister on an outing by the Allegheny River. Although her siblings were considerably older than she, Rachel got along with them well.

they also taught her to be skeptical of big corporations' promises.

Rachel was the youngest of Robert and Maria Carson's three children. Her sister, Marian, was 10 years her senior; her brother, Robert, 8 years older. Because the family lived in a sparsely populated part of town, she had few playmates her own age. But the Carsons were a close-knit family, and Rachel was seldom bored or lonely. In the evening the five of them often sang songs, read books aloud, or discussed current events at the dinner table.

When they were not at school, the Carson children kept busy with farm work during the day. Rachel fed the pigs and horses, gathered the hens' eggs, and milked the cows. Often she churned the milk into butter or used it to make cheese. In the spring she planted the garden; in the summer she weeded. Autumn was the busiest time of the year, for it was then that she

A teacher instructs pupils in an early 20th-century classroom. Aside from her school lessons, Rachel did a great deal of reading on her own.

picked vegetables and apples and stored them for the winter.

But Rachel did not work all the time. Often she would take a break to play with the family's rabbits and cats, or with the dog who usually followed her as she did her chores. Her interest in animals also extended beyond the confines of the farm. "As a child," Carson recalled, "I spent long days out of doors in fields and woods, happiest with the wild birds and creatures as companions."

Rachel's mother had awakened her interest in nature. Maria Carson often took her daughter for walks in the woods, where she taught her the names of the plants, birds, insects, and other animals they encountered. Rachel quickly learned to identify scores of wild things. Maria Carson also encouraged her daughter to develop a reverence for life and a respect for nature's laws. Often, when Mrs. Carson found a bug in the house, she would catch it and carry it outside rather than kill it. Yet she had a practical side that allowed her to tolerate the necessary evil of slaughtering barnyard animals for food. She disliked hunting, but she prepared and cooked the wild rabbits that her son brought home for dinner. And although she loved birds, she accepted that the family cats would kill them. This, after all, was nature's way; it was not for humans to tamper thoughtlessly with the natural order.

Maria Carson also influenced her daughter in another important respect: She taught Rachel to develop her mind and ambitions, even if that meant defying sexual stereotypes. Living in relative isolation on the family farm, Maria could not join in the feminist movement, which then centered on winning the vote for women. But perhaps because she had grown up in an all-female household, or perhaps because society's restrictions had kept her from achieving her own aspirations, she was convinced that women's abilities deserved recognition.

Realizing that her daughter was exceptional in many ways, Mrs. Carson nurtured Rachel's inquisitive mind, sometimes lapsing into overprotectiveness. She took pleasure in Rachel's accomplishments and encouraged her to spend time by herself, reading, writing, and drawing pictures. She was particular about Rachel's companions and preferred that her daughter have a few close friends rather than a wide circle of companions who did not share Rachel's serious interests. Maria Carson was especially concerned about her daughter's health. As a preschooler, Rachel had scarlet fever and was not as robust as other children her age. She was later kept home from school whenever her classmates had colds. But although this special treatment made Rachel something of an

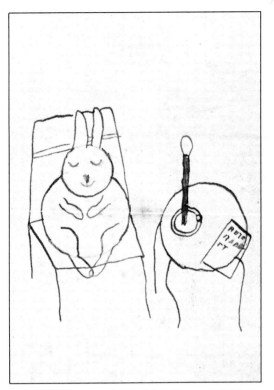

Rachel Carson drew this picture of "A Sleeping Rabbit" when she was 10 years old. One of her favorite books, Peter Rabbit, *lies on the table.*

outsider, it had many benefits. The home environment that Maria Carson created for her daughter was at least as educational and stimulating as the local Springdale public school. Rachel Carson remained close to her mother throughout her life, and it seems that even as a young girl she never resented or rebelled against her mother's high expectations.

Mrs. Carson was much more easygoing with her eldest daughter, Marian, who did not have Rachel's talents.

Rachel and her mother enjoy a quiet moment outdoors. A trained teacher, Maria Carson fostered her daughter's reverence for nature.

Outgoing and very much involved in social activities, Marian introduced her little sister to the popular music and fashions of the time. She later married and had children, seemingly without ever considering the possibility of pursuing a career outside the home. But even early on, it was apparent that Rachel, with her intense curiosity and intellectual concerns, would follow a different path.

In 1917, a month before her 10th birthday, Rachel's peaceful world was shaken. German U-boats (submarines) attacked American merchant vessels carrying supplies to the British and French allies, and the United States entered World War I. Thousands of men were drafted, and the first "doughboys" sailed off to do battle in Europe. A patriotic fever, fanned by a carefully orchestrated propaganda campaign, swept across the United States. Many people supported the war effort out of a love for democracy, but others had less noble motives—and the Wilson administration encouraged these as well. The government released exaggerated accounts of German soldiers' atrocities against European civilians. Conscientious objectors and other opponents of the war were harassed, and many of them were imprisoned. In some parts of the country, American citizens of German ancestry were similarly hounded. Prejudice and intolerance masqueraded as patriotism.

Robert and Maria Carson had always discussed current events with their children, and wartime was no exception. The tone of the family discussions changed from hope to horror, and the focus shifted from local issues to global events. The family shared the country's patriotism, but they were alarmed by the prejudices unleashed by the war.

In school, Rachel learned why the United States was fighting and how civilians, including children, could support the war effort. After her brother Robert joined the U.S. Army Aviation Service, his letters and the stories he told while home on leave inspired Rachel to write a story. Entitled "A Battle in the Clouds," it described the heroism of a Canadian aviator whose plane is hit by German fire. So skillful and daring is this pilot in averting a crash that, out of respect, the Germans stop firing and let him land safely. The most remarkable aspect of Rachel's youthful literary effort was her ability to find humanity on both sides of the conflict. Even though the hero was on the Allied side, Rachel portrayed his adversaries as compassionate human beings—not as ruthless and insensitive killers.

Rachel sent the story to *St. Nicholas* magazine, one of the most popular publications of the time. The magazine featured a special section, the "St. Nicholas League," that printed the literary contributions of young readers. A number of celebrated American writers, including Edna St. Vincent Millay, Stephen Vincent Benét, and Eudora Welty, published their first poems and stories in the "St. Nicholas League." When fourth-grader Rachel Carson joined their ranks, she received the magazine's Silver Badge. "I doubt that any royalty check of recent years has given me as great joy as the notice of that award," Carson commented years later. "Perhaps that early experience of seeing my work in print played its part in fostering my childhood dream of becoming a writer."

She delighted in the whole writing process: imagining a story, putting it on paper, sending it off to a magazine, seeing it in print for everyone to read— and getting paid for the effort. Two more of her stories appeared in *St. Nicholas* before she graduated from

Home on leave, Robert Carson, Jr., visits his sisters. His stories of army life inspired Rachel to write a story published when she was in the fourth grade.

elementary school. One of them, an account of a naval battle during the Spanish-American War of 1898, fused her patriotism with her love of the sea. The other story, which won a Gold Badge for excellence, described the joyful reaction of a group of French soldiers when they learn that the United States has joined the Allied effort in World War I.

Although Rachel's publishing success enhanced her classmates' respect for her, she still stood apart from her peers, both for her shyness and her achievements. As one of her classmates later remarked, her friendships were usually based "not on dates or on being in the same crowd but as an intellectual kind of friendship with highly civilized people." She excelled as a student, maintaining an A average throughout high school.

Rachel did much of her studying not to fulfill course requirements but to satisfy her own curiosity about the world around her. When not at school, doing her chores, or wandering about the forests and fields, she was likely to be immersed in a book. After she had read all the volumes that interested her in the small local public library, she asked family friends to bring her books from Pittsburgh.

Rachel devoured tales of nature and wildlife. As a small girl, she read the Beatrix Potter stories about Peter Rabbit, Jemima Puddle-Duck, and Tom Kitten. When she was still very young, she began to make up her own stories, in which the familiar animals around the farm took on human characteristics. Later, she read the works of Ernest Thompson Seton, one of the most popular nature writers of her time. Seton's stories about forest animals were heroic adventures in which the wild

creatures took on those human characteristics that, he said, reflected "the virtues most admired in Man."

Popular attitudes toward animal life were changing and expanding during Rachel's formative years. When she was in her teens, former President Theodore Roosevelt—a leader of the conservation movement that was just starting up at the time—attacked writ-

Poison gas fells an American soldier as his mask-protected comrades advance on the enemy during World War I. The United States entered the conflict in 1917.

ers like Seton as "nature fakirs." He insisted that stories about nature should describe wild creatures as they really are, because a true understanding of these animals and their environment would enable people to grasp the importance of conserving natural resources.

Appreciating Roosevelt's criticism, Rachel began to favor authors who treated nature realistically and did not attempt to make animal behavior mirror that of human beings. One of her favorite books was *Tarka the Otter*, by British naturalist Henry Williamson. As she later described Williamson's technique: "He enters into the life of the otter, sees with its eyes, follows and portrays the moving drama of its everyday life." She later drew on this realis-

tic approach to nature writing when she wrote her first book, *Under the Sea-Wind*, a 1941 volume that depicted ocean life as perceived by sea creatures.

Much as she enjoyed learning about the fields and forests, Rachel was even more fascinated by another subject. Although Springdale was hundreds of miles inland from the ocean shore, the sea was her favorite reading topic. "I was fascinated by the ocean," Carson later remarked of her early life, "although I had never seen it. I dreamed of it and I longed to see it, and I read all the sea literature I could find."

The books about the ocean that Rachel Carson devoured in her youth were rich in mystery and adventure—tales of pirates, sea monsters, and voyages to exotic lands. These stories sparked her curiosity about mysterious marine creatures and faraway places. For Rachel, the sea was a vast, pristine world where—unlike the Springdale farm—civilization with its industry and pollution would never encroach.

Rachel hungered for detailed knowledge about the marine world, but she found that little was available to her. As she later pointed out in her 1951 book, *The Sea Around Us*, oceanography—the study of the sea—is a relatively new science. Explorers such as Christopher Columbus and Ferdinand Magellan had expanded our knowledge of the ocean's surface in the 15th

Nature writer Ernest Thompson Seton chats with an Indian woman. Rachel eventually came to prefer realistic portrayals of the natural world to Seton's idealized tales.

This fanciful engraving depicts a massive sea serpent. Although she lived hundreds of miles from the coast, Rachel was fascinated by stories about the ocean.

and 16th centuries, but neither they nor the mariners who followed in their wake were able to explore beneath the surface of the sea. Until the 20th century, people did not possess the technology to explore the ocean depths. The underwater world was as much a mystery to scientists during Carson's youth as it was to the sailors of Columbus's time.

But scientists' understanding of the ocean was developing at a rapid pace during the early 20th century. The laying of undersea telegraph and telephone cables linking Europe, Asia, and the Americas, the use of submarines during World War I, and the gradual realization that growing human needs were outpacing the resources of the land all spurred scientific inquiry. As she grew up, Rachel Carson followed the developments in oceanography with great interest. She had found her vocation.

Robert and Maria Carson visit their daughter at the Pennsylvania College for Women in 1925, the year that Carson began studying at the Pittsburgh institution.

THREE

To the Sea

The United States had entered a period known as the Roaring Twenties or the Jazz Age when 18-year-old Rachel Carson left Springdale to attend the Pennsylvania College for Women. The nation had changed remarkably during the past several years. The end of World War I in November 1918 had ushered in a new morality that encouraged personal freedom and youthful frivolity.

It was an era of flappers, bootleg whiskey, ragtime music, and such popular dances as the tango, Charleston, and turkey trot. Prohibition (the ban on the manufacture and sale of alcoholic drinks) had been in effect since 1920. Yet thousands ignored the law and frequented illegal saloons known as speakeasies. For the first time, many young women from "respectable" homes cut their hair short and went out on dates without adult chaperons.

The decade had opened with the passage of the 19th amendment, which granted women the right to vote, but the 1920s were marked by widespread political conservatism. The drive for social reform, which included such feminist demands as equal rights and equal opportunity, lost momentum as the public seemed to turn away from political action in favor of pursuing blissful good times.

Carson had more serious goals in mind when she entered the Pennsylvania College for Women (now Chatham College) in 1925. She lived away from home in a dormitory, but her independence was by no means complete: On weekends either Carson went home or her mother came to visit the school's Pittsburgh campus. Because of her studiousness and her

A flapper does the Charleston, a dance popular during the Roaring Twenties. Carson was more interested in her studies than in the frivolity that marked the era.

ing and nature. She had a good sense of humor and enjoyed spending time with her friends. But as always, she was content on her own, studying, reading, and writing. She wrote several stories, mostly about the sea, for the college literary magazine; she also wrote poems, which she kept to herself.

Carson entered college still intent on becoming a writer. In an essay written during her first month at school, Carson named Samuel Clemens, who wrote under the pen name Mark Twain, as her favorite American author. "His philosophy, humor, and straightforward hatred of hypocrisy," she wrote, "have touched a responsive chord in my heart." Carson's goal was to follow in his footsteps, using her prose to illuminate the joys and follies of the human condition.

During her sophomore year, however, Carson took a biology course taught by a dynamic young teacher, Mary Scott Skinker. The field trips to the woods, cliffs, and waterways of western Pennsylvania reminded Carson of her tramps around the Springdale farm. Work in the biology laboratory examining familiar plants and animals under a microscope sparked her intellectual curiosity. She had always been observant of nature, but now she was perceiving it anew, through the prism of a scientific discipline. Her expanding understanding of the way nature worked heightened her

close relationship with her mother, Carson stood out at college, much as she had in Springdale.

Although she chose to lead a quiet life devoted to her studies, Carson was not a hermit. She worked on the college newspaper, joined the literary club, dated occasionally, and played goalie on an intramural field hockey team. She befriended a number of teachers and students—especially those who shared her interests in writ-

Carson (back row, second from right) joins the other members of her college field hockey team for a group portrait that appeared in her school yearbook.

love of the outdoors. Carson enjoyed the company of the other biology students as well. She and Mary Skinker became good friends as their shared interest in the natural world erased the barrier separating student and teacher.

Carson's decision to switch her major from English to biology drew opposition from her other teachers and the college administration. Society had for the most part accepted women as writers, and Carson's teachers were confi-

dent that she had the talent to succeed in that field. They also reasoned that even if she could not make a living as a writer, she could always teach English, one of the few academic fields that then welcomed women. Science, on the other hand, was a closed fraternity. Other than teaching jobs at women's colleges, the field offered women virtually no opportunities. Carson had no idea that she might fuse the two disciplines that interested her: "I thought I had to be one or the other; it never

Carson enjoys an informal discussion with a professor. Biology teacher Mary Skinker's influence was a factor in Carson's decision to change her major from English to biology.

occurred to me, or apparently to anyone else, that I could combine the two careers."

Science became her college major and primary focus, writing her avocation. In her junior and senior years, she filled her schedule with biology, zoology, and other science courses. She continued to write—something she always felt a need to do—and in her senior year began submitting poems to national publications. The poems have never been found, but Carson saved her rejection slips for posterity.

Because of her family's declining economic fortunes (her father was unable to sell enough building lots to pay for her education), Carson needed a small scholarship to help meet her expenses. When even this proved insufficient, the president and dean of the college solicited contributions from their personal friends. Carson was one of the school's prized students, and no one in the administration wanted her to drop out for lack of money. Nonetheless, Carson had to take out additional loans from the college in order to complete her schooling. In 1929 she graduated magna cum laude (with high honors). On the recommendation of the administration and faculty, she was awarded a full scholarship at prestigious Johns Hopkins University in Baltimore, Maryland, to study for a master's degree in marine zoology.

The summer before she entered Johns Hopkins, Carson spent six weeks as an intern (or, as the staff put it, a "beginning investigator") at Woods Hole Marine Biological Laboratory. Located on Cape Cod in Massachusetts, the lab was the center for oceanic research on North America's Atlantic coast. In late July Carson boarded a train that would take her, for the first time in her life, to the sea. It was a rainy summer day when she set sail from New York City for Woods Hole, but she stood on the deck as the boat rounded the tip of Manhattan, passed the Statue of Liberty, and turned north toward Long Island Sound and the high sea. She could see the ocean at last.

Carson's experiences at Woods Hole, where she was "almost literally surrounded by the ocean," fueled her desire to become a marine zoologist. The creatures of the sea fascinated her, as did the ocean itself. Though she spent much of her time dissecting fish in a laboratory, she also found opportunities to wander along the rocky shore examining the plants and animals she had long read about in books

In 1929 Carson graduated from the Pennsylvania College for Women. The faculty of her alma mater recommended her for a scholarship, enabling her to go on to graduate school.

but had never seen before. Carson, who felt her "destiny was somehow linked with the sea" even before she laid eyes on it, found her first encounters with the ocean exhilarating. Just sitting on the beach watching and listening to the shore birds, observing the tides, and feeling the sting of the salt air against her skin was the fulfillment of a lifelong dream.

Carson was 22 when she first saw the sea while on her way to the Woods Hole Marine Biological Laboratory, a Cape Cod, Massachusetts, center for ocean research.

Woods Hole staffers picnic on the dunes in the summer of 1929. Carson enjoyed the companionship of men and women who shared her interest in science and the sea.

Years later, Carson wrote about Woods Hole and the importance of that first summer by the sea:

> There I could see the racing tidal currents pouring through the "Hole" or watch the waves breaking at Nobska Point after a storm, and there I first became really aware of the unseen ocean currents, for masses of drifting sargassum weed would come in from the distant Gulf Stream after a storm, and tropical creatures like the beautiful Portuguese man-of-war were carried in from the warm rivers offshore.

Carson also reveled in the company of her fellow scientists. Up until then, her intellectual interests had more or less marked her as a loner. But at Woods Hole she discovered a community of people who shared a passion for science and the sea. After work, they often gathered—at a picnic on the beach or over coffee in the dining hall—to share their theories, aspirations, and delight in working and living in so interesting an environment. Rachel Carson had found her niche.

Rachel Carson moved to Baltimore, Maryland, in 1929 when she entered Johns Hopkins University to study for her master's degree in marine zoology.

FOUR

"Something to Write About"

On her way to Baltimore to begin her studies at Johns Hopkins in September 1929, Carson stopped off in Washington, D.C. She took the detour in order to pay a call on Elmer Higgins, the head of the Division of Scientific Inquiry at the Bureau of Fisheries of the United States Department of Commerce. Higgins, she had heard, was a sensitive man who always kept his door open to young scientists. Never reluctant to call on experts when she needed information, Carson wanted to ask him what opportunities might be available to her after graduate school and what courses she should take to prepare herself. A frank man, Higgins told her what others had already warned her about: Besides teaching, there were few jobs open to female scientists. Industry did not hire women in professional capacities; nei-

ther did museums or research institutions. Natural scientists often performed fieldwork under conditions that the male scientific establishment considered "too rugged" for women. There was the possibility of government work, Higgins suggested, but the government was not hiring at the time. Even if it had been, Higgins did not know of any woman working for the government in a position higher than that of secretary or clerical worker.

The issue of sexual discrimination in Carson's chosen field would soon be overshadowed by global events. In October 1929, two months after she began her graduate studies, the bottom fell out of the U.S. stock market. This crash precipitated a worldwide depression that destroyed the American economy and shattered the dreams and ambitions of many young people of Car-

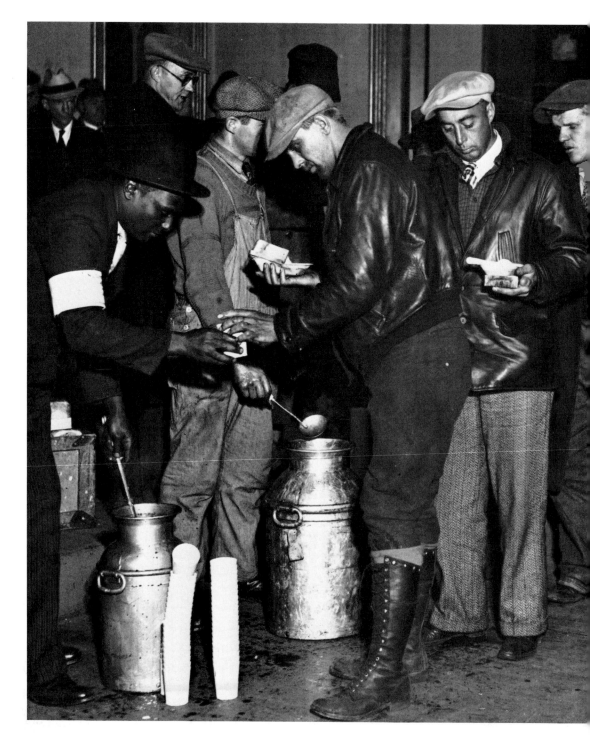

son's generation. As factories closed and businesses failed, millions lost their jobs. Unemployment in the United States rose from 1.5 million to 12.1 million. At the height of the Great Depression as many as 15 million Americans—nearly one-third of the work force—were jobless. With her full scholarship, Carson was able to remain in school. But she was well aware that when she graduated she would face tremendous odds: Jobs for marine biologists—men and women alike— were virtually nonexistent.

Nevertheless, Carson continued her studies, earning her usual high grades. Some of her professors helped her find part-time work teaching at Johns Hopkins and the University of Maryland. She spent her summers teaching at Johns Hopkins and working at Woods Hole. In 1932 she received her master's degree in marine zoology, but other than her summer job at Johns Hopkins, she had no work—and her prospects looked grim.

During the Depression it was common for young adults and their parents to pool their resources and share housing. While Carson was still in school, Robert and Maria Carson abandoned their Springdale home and moved into their daughter's tiny

Men line up to receive a free meal during the Great Depression. Like millions of other Americans, Carson's job prospects were bleak during this period.

This photograph of a Johns Hopkins biology class (circa 1930) demonstrates that Carson was entering a male-dominated field when she decided to pursue a science career.

rented cottage, which was a 30-minute trolley ride away from Johns Hopkins. The Carson home became even more crowded in 1933 when Robert, Jr., moved in briefly after losing his job. Fortunately, he soon found work repairing radios and was able to help support the family.

Money was in such short supply those days that many of Robert Carson's repairs were done for barter. One woman gave him a cat in exchange for his fixing her radio. Rachel Carson loved cats, so "Mitzie" became a permanent part of the household. As they

had been in her childhood, pets were important to Carson; she would always have at least one pet for the rest of her life.

The Carsons' group effort to weather the Great Depression received a staggering setback on July 6, 1935, when Robert Carson, Sr., died suddenly. Saddened by the loss of her father, Carson found consolation exploring the shore of nearby Chesapeake Bay. But she could not give in to her sorrow—she realized that she absolutely had to find a full-time job.

By this time, her employment prospects did not seem as bleak as they had when she graduated. Three years earlier, Franklin Delano Roosevelt had been elected president on his promise to give the beleaguered American people a "New Deal." His predecessor in the White House, Herbert Hoover, had waited expectantly for the economy to right itself after the stock market crash, but Roosevelt believed that government intervention was the only way to revive the sluggish U.S. economy. His administration stepped in to help the unemployed by giving them jobs on federally funded public work projects. Thousands were hired to build new roads, bridges, harbors, dams, schools, and hospitals.

Roosevelt and his advisers were convinced that these new jobs would not only benefit the individuals who filled them but also revive the economy as a whole. The theory was that people with jobs would spend their paychecks on goods and services. This increased demand would in turn create new jobs, as private industry increased production to satisfy new consumers. By "priming the pump" in the public sector, the federal government hoped to rejuvenate the entire national economy. Like his distant cousin, former president Theodore Roosevelt, the current president was an enthusiastic conservationist, and many of the jobs created during the New Deal era involved protecting natural resources. Carson and others like

President Roosevelt's Civilian Conservation Corps and other programs employed men and women during the depression.

her felt more hopeful about the future as jobs opened up and conservation became a government priority.

The New Deal also encouraged employers to take a new attitude toward women. President Roosevelt's wife, Eleanor, emerged as a powerful advocate of social justice, including the rights of women. The president himself broke precedent by appointing Frances Perkins secretary of labor, making her the first woman in American history to hold a cabinet post. Opportunities for women were still limited, and unemployment was still the country's number one problem, but attitudes—at least in the federal

In 1935 Elmer Higgins, an official at the U.S. Bureau of Fisheries, hired Carson to write scripts for a radio program about marine life.

for a weekly radio series about marine life. The series' title was "Romance Under the Waters," but the staff humorously called the show "Seven-Minute Fish Tales." Higgins had initially hired a professional writer to do the scripts, but the writer knew nothing about the subject and quickly ran out of ideas. The scientists on his staff then took up the task, but none of them knew how to produce radio scripts that were both informative and entertaining. As Carson recalled later, Higgins was desperate. "I've never seen a written word of yours," he told her, "but I'm going to take a sporting chance."

Although Carson had continued to write poetry (which still went unpublished), she had, by this time, abandoned the idea of writing for a living. But Higgins's job description suited her interests perfectly. She knew nothing about radio scriptwriting, but she was confident of her writing ability. Her first task was to produce three trial assignments, which paid $19.25 each. Pleased by her work, Higgins hired her as a part-time writer for $1,000 a year.

Carson's scripts were so well written that Higgins eventually asked her to "produce something of a general sort about the sea." She later remarked that as she was working on this vague assignment "the material rather took charge of the situation and turned into something that was, perhaps, unusual as a broadcast for the Commissioner of

government—were changing. Jobs once barred to women were now opening up.

Heartened by these changes, Carson traveled to Washington to call on Elmer Higgins a second time. Seven years had passed since her first visit to the Bureau of Fisheries, but Higgins had not forgotten the shy yet forthright woman who had impressed him with her determination to make science her career. This time fortune was on her side. Higgins's department had been assigned the task of producing a script

"Undersea," Carson's article describing the rich array of life below the ocean's surface, was published by the Atlantic Monthly *in 1937.*

Fisheries." She reported that when Higgins read her piece, he "handed it back with a twinkle in his eye. 'I don't think it will do,' he said. 'Better try again. But send this one to the *Atlantic*.'" Carson followed his advice: She wrote something simpler for the bureau and sent her more ambitious work off to the *Atlantic Monthly*. One of the foremost literary magazines in the country, the *Atlantic* had a reputation for publishing the work of conservation advocates. Carson hoped to join their ranks.

The conflict that Carson felt between writing and pursuing a career in science resolved itself when she realized that she could successfully use her literary skills to communicate information about nature. Carson had discovered a specialty that would soon become her life's work. She later recalled, "It dawned on me that by becoming a biologist I had given myself something to write about."

In 1936 Carson took the exam required to apply for an entry-level civil service post as a junior aquatic biologist. The only woman taking the test, Carson earned the highest score and became the second woman hired in a full-time professional capacity by the

Fishermen haul in their nets. The only human character in Under the Sea-Wind *was a fisherman who, like Carson herself, was awed by the ocean's mysteries.*

U.S. Bureau of Fisheries. At Elmer Higgins's request, Carson was assigned to his office, where she answered public inquiries about fish and other marine life. Much of this work involved tracking down the existing research on requested topics and explaining what she had found in language that nonscientists could understand. Her job exposed her to every aspect of oceanography, enabling her to develop her knowledge of a wide range of aquatic life.

Shortly after Carson landed her government job and moved to Silver Spring, Maryland, her sister, Marian, died. Marian's two preteen daughters, Virginia and Marjorie Williams, joined the Carson household. Maria Carson kept house and cared for the children, and Rachel became the breadwinner for the four of them.

"Undersea," the piece that she had sent to the *Atlantic*, was published in 1937. Carson was elated by her success, especially when she began receiving a stream of letters from men and women who complimented her on her prose and expressed enthusiasm for the mysterious world to which Carson had introduced them. Hendrik Willem van Loon, the author of a widely popular book called *The Story of Mankind*, was one of these admirers. He invited Carson to visit him and his wife at their Connecticut home. There, he told her that during a recent trip across the Atlantic he had been impressed by its seeming lifelessness—"Not a snout nor a spout did I see." Carson's essay, he told her, had opened his eyes to the rich variety of life that existed under the ocean's surface. Van Loon's editor, Quincy Howe, had also been intrigued by the *Atlantic* piece, and Carson met with him during her visit to Connecticut. Howe told her that his publishing company, Simon and Schuster, wanted her to produce a volume on ocean life. Surprised and pleased by Howe's offer, Carson "went home to start work on the book which everyone seemed to think I should write."

Under the Sea-Wind, Carson's first book, was three years in the making. Carson worked on weekends and at night, often writing into the early morning hours before putting in a full day at her government job. When it was published in 1941, Carson spelled out her goal for the book in its preface: "To make the sea and its life as vivid a reality for those who may read the book as it has become for me during the past decade."

In the three stories that make up *Under the Sea-Wind*, the reader encounters a vivid array of marine creatures locked in life-and-death struggles as they carry out nature's dictates. Carson's narrative follows a family of shorebirds on their migration from North America to their Arctic nesting place, where the winter is harsh and they barely survive. The book also describes the adventures of a mackerel,

One night the mackerel came upon an abandoned gill net swaying in the water. The net was buoyed at the surface by cork floats; and from the cork line it hung down ~~perpendicularly~~ — ~~it~~ like a giant tennis net. Its meshes were 2 inches across so that the yearling mackerel could have slipped through, although larger ~~ones~~ would have been gilled in the twine. Tonight no fish would have tried to pass through the net, for all its meshes were hung with tiny warning lamps. ~~the~~ ~~bodies of the myriad luminescent animals of the the wet twine in the dark sea + the pulse of the ocean stirred from them~~ _Peridinium, and Ceratium and — ; Noctiluca —_ clung to _being a thousand thousand meeting sparks of light_ It was as though all the myriad lesser fry of the sea, the animals small as a dust mote the plants tinier than a _____ drifting ~~endlessly~~ _from birth to death_ in ocean, ~~infinitely long~~ _without end or beginning for them. (endlessly fluid)_ seized upon the meshes of the gill net as the one firm _____ in their fluid world. and clung to it with protoplasmic hair and cilia, with tentacle and _____. The gill net glowed like a thing alive; its radiance shone out into the ~~black~~ black sea, shone down into the darkness below, and _brought_ ~~drew~~ up amphipods and — + — drawn by the light, and these larger creatures also clung to the meshes. ~~So~~ the net gave _____ to

This page from a draft of Carson's first book, Under the Sea-Wind, bears a sketch of the author's beloved pet cat.

Above all, *Under the Sea-Wind* is a dramatic portrayal of the principles of ecology, an examination of the way in which different species depend on one another. In one episode a shark attacks a channel bass that had recently eaten a ghost crab that had fed in turn on beach fleas. The remains of the bass wash up on the shore as food for the fleas. For the creatures who live in and around the sea, life is a continuous battle for survival: against the tides, the weather, and human and nonhuman adversaries. Individual creatures die to assure the survival of the species, Carson explained; with death, the cycle of life continues.

People are the ultimate predators in Carson's ocean world, but fishing is portrayed as a necessity because it provides human beings with food. The only human character in *Under the Sea-Wind* is a young fisherman. Perhaps he is meant to reflect Carson's point of view, for he is filled with "wonder" and "unslakable curiosity" about life under the surface of the sea. Hauling in a net full of mackerel, he studies the fishes' eyes, speculating about what they had seen in the dark and unfathomable ocean world that he, as a human, would never see: "It seemed to him incongruous that a creature that had made a go of life in the sea, that had run the gauntlet of all the relentless enemies that he knew roved through that dimness his eyes could not penetrate, should at last

Dr. William Beebe confers with his staff. One of the few marine scientists interested in helping women advance in the field, Beebe had high praise for Carson's writing.

which escapes the deadly sting of a jelly comb and the snare of a trawler's net only to be attacked by a school of tuna, who are themselves driven off by the arrival of killer whales. Exhausted from its struggle, the mackerel instinctively makes its way to its spawning ground far beneath the ocean's surface, "a place he had never known." These and dozens of other creatures appear in the book, illustrating Carson's point that the ocean is many things: a nursery, a battleground, and a microcosm of life itself.

come to death on the deck of a mackerel seiner [a fishing boat], slimy with fish gurry and slippery with scales." *Under the Sea-Wind* was a resounding critical success. "There is drama in every sentence," one newspaper reviewer wrote. "She rouses our interest in this ocean world and we want to watch it." Even more satisfying, in Carson's eyes, was the acclaim the book received from other scientists. Dr. William Beebe, who in 1934 became the first person to probe the ocean depths when he descended more than a half-mile below the Atlantic in a round steel craft called a "bathysphere," declared that "Miss Carson's science cannot be questioned." A few years later, he included parts of her book in his own *The Book of Naturalists*. Beebe's anthology opened with the observations of the ancient Greek philosopher Aristotle and concluded with excerpts from Carson's work. Carson was one of only two women to have their work included in the book.

For the rest of her life, *Under the Sea-Wind* remained Carson's favorite work, but her first book was a financial disaster despite the critics' praise. Years later, she noted wryly that "The world received the event with superb indifference." Less than a month after its publication in November 1941, the Japanese attacked Pearl Harbor and the United States was plunged into

Smoke billows from U.S. ships after the Japanese bombing of Pearl Harbor in 1941, an act that precipitated America's entry into World War II.

World War II. Carson's lyrical ode to the ocean's majesty would be largely ignored by a public engrossed in the war effort. Only 1,600 copies of the book sold during the next six years. But the Second World War, like the first, would contribute to humanity's understanding of Carson's favorite subject: the sea. The United States had entered a war fought on and under two oceans, and research into the sea became a national priority.

Carson's dog patiently models his owner's sunglasses while the biologist relaxes on the steps of her Silver Spring, Maryland, home.

FIVE

The Sea Becomes a Best-Seller

Never in its history had the United States been as united in common cause as it was during the Second World War. The entire country mobilized to defeat the Axis powers, Germany, Italy, and Japan. Soldiers streamed to battlefronts in Europe and the Pacific, while at home civilians did their part, saving scrap metal, buying war bonds, and planting "victory gardens."

Oceanographers played an important role during the conflict. In order to wage battle on the Pacific islands and along the European coast, the United States and its allies had to perfect their ability to navigate the seas and bring soldiers, weapons, and supplies ashore on enemy-held beaches.

The establishment of European beachheads and the island-hopping campaign in the Pacific could not have been accomplished without detailed knowledge of ocean currents and coastal tides. Submarine crews needed accurate information on water depth and the topography of the ocean bottom. Their lives depended on knowledge of factors such as the location of undersea canyons where they—or their enemies—could wait in ambush.

By the time the United States entered World War II in 1941, Rachel Carson had become an important figure in the U.S. Fish and Wildlife Service, a recently created federal organization that had absorbed the Bureau of Fisheries. Promotions came rapidly, and in

1942 she was made assistant to the chief of the office of information. As she wrote and edited government publications, virtually all the new research in oceanography crossed her desk: recently charted maps of the ocean depths, reports on the nutritional value of fish and other sea products, discoveries of mineral resources under the ocean floor, and studies of animal behavior and intelligence.

During the war, Carson was too busy to find much time for her own writing. She did manage to produce a few short pieces, and in 1944 the *Reader's Digest* printed an article she had written on bats. "The Bat Knew It First" described how the invention of radar had its basis in research into the way bats use sound waves to "see" in the dark. The article was widely reprinted and used by the navy in its recruitment drives.

Carson's government job was not without its frustrations. In 1942 she and her family were forced to relocate to Chicago, Illinois, when the Fish and Wildlife Service moved out of Washington because of a shortage of office space there. When she returned to the capital after a year in the Midwest, Carson found her job increasingly exhausting. "I'm definitely in the mood to make a change of some sort," she wrote to a friend, "preferably to something that will give me more time for my own writing. At this stage, that

seems the prime necessity." She applied for positions at the *Reader's Digest*, the New York Zoological Society, and the National Audubon Society, but was turned down by all three.

Nonetheless, Carson kept her spirits up. As a co-worker later reported, Carson's "zest and humor made even the dull stretches of bureaucratic procedure a matter for quiet fun, and she could instill a sense of adventure into the editorial routine of a government department." Although she longed to have more time for her own writing projects, Carson knew her government work was worthwhile. Washington, D.C., was an exciting place during the war years, as men and women from all over the country flooded into the capital to help manage the war effort. There was a comradeship among government workers—a belief that what they were doing was important for the future of the country—that Carson shared.

Carson's private life during this period centered on her family and colleagues. She spent much of her time with her nieces or helping her mother with household tasks. She also found

As America fought a two-ocean war, information on tides, currents, and the surface of the seafloor became vitally important in planning troop landings and submarine routes.

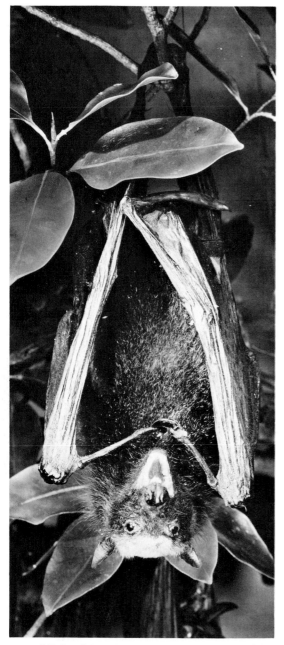

Published in 1944, Carson's article "The Bat Knew It First" described the way in which bats' ability to "see" with sound waves led to the development of radar.

time to become active in the local Audubon Society, joining other government workers for early morning bird-watching expeditions in city parks and along the banks of the Potomac River. In the evenings, she often attended parties held by her colleagues. One of her co-workers, Shirley Briggs, later remarked that "Rachel appreciated so many kinds of people, and was always glad to meet new ones and enter into whatever conversation or merriment was going on at these affairs."

After the war, the Fish and Wildlife Service tried to revive the New Deal's spirit of conservationism. In 1949 Carson became editor-in-chief for all of the department's publications. One of her pet projects was the production of 12 booklets entitled "Conservation in Action." The purpose of the pamphlets was to educate the public about the importance of conserving natural resources, including plant life and wild animals. In her introduction to the series, she wrote: "Wild creatures, like men, must have a place to live. As civilization creates cities, builds highways, and drains marshes, it takes away, little by little, the land that is suitable for wildlife. And as their spaces for living dwindle, the wildlife populations themselves decline." Carson was committed to reversing this trend, but the conservation movement was politically weak at this time and the objectives of the Fish and Wildlife Service were often ignored.

Carson's frustration with her job resurfaced, but once again, despite her impressive qualifications, the private sector was not yet ready to hire a female scientist. Carson continued working for the government, but at the same time, she began work on a second book, *The Sea Around Us*.

Her goal for this volume was nothing if not ambitious: She wanted to write an easily understandable yet scientifically accurate book on the sea that incorporated the extensive oceanographic research done during the war. "I am impressed by man's dependence upon the ocean, directly, and in thousands of ways unsuspected by most people," she wrote to a friend as she embarked on the project. "These relationships, and my belief that we will become even more dependent upon the ocean as we destroy the land, are really the themes of this book."

She began work in 1948, writing at what she considered to be an agonizingly slow pace. Besides simply finding enough time to work on her project, one of her problems was perfectionism as she struggled to make her prose match the beauty and wonder that she found in ocean life. But, as she would later recall, "the backbone of the work was just plain hard slogging—searching in the often dry and exceedingly technical papers of scientists for the kernels of fact to weld into my profile of the sea. I believe I consulted, at a minimum, somewhat more than a

Among Carson's contributions to the war effort were pamphlets encouraging Americans to eat more fish in order to conserve meat for consumption by U.S. troops.

thousand separate printed sources. In addition to this, I corresponded with oceanographers all over the world and personally discussed the book with many specialists."

One of the experts she consulted was Dr. Beebe, the underwater explorer, who told her, "You can't write

Her diving helmet at her feet, Carson examines the Florida coastline. Researching The Sea Around Us, *Carson explored the region's coral reefs in 1949.*

this book until you have gotten your head under water." Taking his advice, Carson donned a diver's helmet in July 1949 and explored the reefs off the Florida Keys to a depth of 15 feet. The variety of fish and the complexity of the coral forms astonished her. For the first time, she said, "I learned what the surface of the water looks like underneath and how exquisitely delicate and varied are the colors displayed by the animals of the reef, and I got the feeling of the misty green vistas of a strange, nonhuman world."

The following month Carson had another marine adventure. One of her duties at the Fish and Wildlife Service was to distribute information on the bureau's research ship, the *Albatross III*. As she wryly noted, "It was decided finally—and I might have had something to do with originating the idea—that perhaps I could do a better job of handling publications about the *Albatross* if I had been out on her." Carson and her literary agent, Marie Rodell, became the first women to join the 50-member crew of the *Albatross III*. On that trip, the ship cruised the North Atlantic waters of Georges Bank off the coast of Nova Scotia. Its mission was to gather information on a recent drop in the population of several of the area's valuable commercial fish species. For more than a week Carson observed as the ship's crew took depth surveys and studied the fish captured in the vessel's huge trawler nets.

Part fishing boat and part science lab, the *Albatross III* exposed Carson to a world dominated by the sights, smells, and sounds of the open sea. In the ship's laboratory she worked with biologists examining varied forms of sea life under microscopes. On deck she heard machines groan as powerful winches dragged up nets full of fish. And in the operations room she watched depth recorders chart the ocean terrain and heard the echo of sonar (a device that used sound waves to detect objects under water) as it bounced off schools of fish. The ship's crew was initially wary of the women on board, but they quickly came to respect their seriousness and Carson's quiet but confident scientific knowledge. For her part, Carson's voyage on the *Albatross III* heightened her enthusiasm for her book on the ocean.

A research grant enabled Carson to take an unpaid leave-of-absence from work, and she completed her manuscript in 1950. *The Sea Around Us* told the story of the world's oceans from their origins billions of years ago to the modern era. The book explored the sea from its surface to its depths: its currents and tides; its plants, fish, and microscopic animal life; its place in human history; and its future as an untapped natural resource. *The Sea Around Us* wove together the disciplines of biology, zoology, and geology. Carson also drew on seafaring history, mythology, and folk tales. Although

In 1949 Carson and her literary agent became the first women to board the Albatross III, *the Fish and Wildlife Service's research vessel.*

she had worked on the manuscript for less than three years, the book was really the culmination of her lifelong fascination with the sea. "I have been collecting material for this ocean book all my life," she told a friend. "My mind has stored up everything I have ever learned about it as well as my own thoughts, impressions, and emotions."

Portions of the upcoming book appeared in several magazines, including the *Yale Review, Science Digest*, and *Vogue*. One of these excerpts earned Carson an award from the American Association for the Advancement of Science as the "finest example of science writing in any American magazine in 1950." After the *New Yorker* condensed the book into a three-part

"Profile of the Sea," the magazine was flooded with complimentary letters. Unable to believe that a woman could be such an accomplished scientist, one male admirer wrote, "I assume from the author's knowledge that he must be a man."

Despite this early acclaim, neither the author nor her publisher was prepared for the book's success. Carson was not a well-known writer at the time, and the sea was not a typical subject for literary best-sellers. Yet soon after *The Sea Around Us* came out on July 2, 1951, it climbed onto the *New York Times* best-seller list—and stayed there for a record 86 weeks. According to one critic, "Once or twice in a generation does the world get a

Coral is composed of the external skeletons of sea creatures. Carson's The Sea Around Us *describes the ocean from its surface to its depths.*

physical scientist with literary genius. Miss Carson has written a classic in *The Sea Around Us.*" Because of the book's universal appeal, it was eventually translated into 32 languages.

The Sea Around Us and its author both received many awards and honors. Carson's latest work was named "outstanding book of the year" in the *New York Times* annual Christmas poll, and won the John Burroughs Medal for a nature book of high literary merit.

Carson received honorary degrees from Smith College, Oberlin College, Drexel Institute of Technology, and Chatham College, her alma mater. From Great Britain came news that she had been elected a Fellow of the Royal Society of Literature, and shortly thereafter she was elected to the National Institute of Arts and Letters, making her the second woman to receive the United States's most prestigious literary honor. But Carson was modest about all the ac-

Along with poet Marianne Moore and novelist James Jones, Carson received the National Book Award for 1951. The Sea Around Us *earned her the prize for nonfiction.*

claim bestowed on her. "If there is poetry in my book about the sea," she said upon receiving the National Book Award for the best nonfiction book of 1951, "it is not because I put it there but because no one could write truthfully about the sea and leave out the poetry."

Hollywood took notice as well. A major studio, RKO, bought the movie rights to *The Sea Around Us* but ignored Carson's advice on how it should be filmed. Although Carson considered the adaptation melodramatic and disdainful of fact, it won an Oscar for the best full-length documentary of 1953. After this movie fiasco, she was careful about lending her name to projects she could not control

or was not personally enthusiastic about.

The author of *The Sea Around Us* was uneasy in the public spotlight. A bemused and somewhat overwhelmed Carson reported that several months after the book's publication she was sitting under the hair dryer in a beauty parlor—a place "which until then I had considered an inviolate sanctuary"—when the owner came over, turned off the dryer, and insisted that Carson greet one of her fans. Incidents like this were all too common, prompting her to complain that "what has gone on in the last six months is all very fine, but enough is enough!"

Although Carson's celebrity deprived her of privacy, it also brought

Carson collects specimens with the illustrator of The Edge of the Sea. *Uncomfortable with her celebrity status, she was happiest doing fieldwork.*

Carson took this photograph of the pounding surf near her summer retreat in Maine. She bought the house with proceeds from her best-selling books on the sea.

her many opportunities. Her publishing success enabled her to leave her government job and become a full-time writer, traveling and doing field research on her own. She embarked on several projects and was even asked to write the album notes for celebrated conductor Arturo Toscanini's recording of Claude Debussy's *La Mer* (*The Sea*), one of her favorite musical compositions.

In 1952 the success of *The Sea Around Us* led to the reissue of *Under the Sea-Wind*. This time around, the book received not only critical acclaim but the public's enthusiasm as well. Her first book joined *The Sea Around Us* on the *New York Times* best-seller list. As the newspaper pointed out, Carson's dual triumph was a "publishing phenomenon rare as a total solar eclipse."

With the proceeds from her books, Carson bought land on the rocky coast of Maine and built a summer cottage. There, with the sound of the sea as a constant companion, she spent her happiest times. She examined nearby tidal pools with neighbors who shared her love of the ocean. Often, she would take live specimens home for study under a microscope before returning them to the sea, carefully placing them exactly where she found them.

Inspired by her coastal investigations, Carson began work on her next book, *The Edge of the Sea*. The work would explore North America's Atlantic coast from the coral reefs and mangrove swamps of the Florida Everglades to the rocky cliffs and coves near her Maine home. More than a description of the variety of life that inhabits the shoreline, the finished book also illuminates the ecology of shore life. Carson eloquently illustrates the way in which the survival of shore plants and animals such as barnacles, seaweed, and mussels depends on one another and on the surf, tides, and climate. She wrote that her goal in writing the book was "to interpret the shore in terms of that essential unity that binds life to the earth."

Exploring the many manifestations of this unity, *The Edge of the Sea* travels back into geologic time to explain why the shoreline looks as it does and how the plants and animals that live in this "border zone" between water and land have evolved into their present forms. "To understand the life

of the shore," Carson wrote, "it is not enough to pick up an empty shell and say 'This is a murex,' or 'That is an angel wing.' " Instead, she traced the life of the creature that once inhabited the empty shell: "How it survived amid surf and storm, what were its enemies, how it found food and reproduced its kind, what were its relations to the particular sea world in which it lived."

The Edge of the Sea was published in 1955, first as a series in the *New Yorker* and then in book form. Like her other books, it was praised by critics and became a best-seller. Rachel Carson was now at the top of her profession. Her professional peers held her in highest regard, her books had made her a household name, and publishers clamored for her work.

But as Carson herself had said, "No writer can stand still." During the next few years she would work on a variety of topics, expanding her range both as a scientist and a writer. In the summer of 1956 Carson wrote a magazine article about helping children to appreciate nature. The piece was based on her own experiences with her four-year-old grandnephew Roger, whom she often took on jaunts along the rugged shore near her summer home in Maine. The article, which was later published in book form under the title *The Sense of Wonder*, portrayed the natural world as a wondrous delight, especially as seen through the innocent, enthusiastic eyes of a child:

Carson once remarked that "The discipline of the writer is to learn to be still and listen to what his subject has to tell him."

A child's world is fresh and new and beautiful, full of wonder and excitement. It is our misfortune that for most of us that clear-eyed vision, that true instinct for what is beautiful and awe-inspiring, is dimmed and even lost before we reach adulthood. If I had influence with the good fairy who is supposed to preside over the christening of all children I should ask that her gift to each child in the world be a sense of wonder so indestructible that it would last throughout life, as an unfailing antidote against the boredom and disenchantments of later years, the sterile preoccupation with things that are artificial, the alienation from the sources of our strength.

Carson hoped that she would be able to carry the positive theme of *The Sense of Wonder* over into her next book, in which she planned to explore the human race's relationship with nature. But the article's upbeat theme did not reflect her growing pessimism about humanity's widespread—and dangerous—alienation from nature. In the next several years, Carson would see more and more evidence of the inexorable progress of this trend. Fearful that human beings were severing their connection with the natural order, she began laying the groundwork for her next book, a massive undertaking that would change her life—and the world around her.

As Carson considered writing about humanity's place in the natural order, she felt the urgent need to warn her readers of the dangers of damaging the environment.

SIX

Confronting the Truth

For her next major project, Carson envisioned a work with a broad ecological theme. She wanted to write a book that would describe the interrelationship between human beings and the natural environment—one that would sum up her belief in the balance of nature and the sanctity of life. Her growing awareness of disturbing trends in recent government policy added an urgency to the project and made Carson realize that her next book could not be just a celebration of life. She had to sound a warning.

In 1952 Republican Dwight D. Eisenhower had been elected president. His administration reduced the federal government's regulation of the economy and reversed the conservation policies inaugurated during the New Deal. The man Eisenhower chose as his secretary of the interior, a former

used-car salesman named Douglas McKay, dismissed conservationists as "long-haired punks." Along with the new secretary of agriculture, Ezra Taft Benson, McKay wanted to minimize federal regulation of natural resources and give lumber companies, mining corporations, fishing fleets, and large farming concerns greater access to the forests, parks, grazing lands, and waterways that the federal government had been protecting.

Under McKay's direction, many of the government's more conservation-minded administrators and scientists—Carson's colleagues from her days in the civil service—were dismissed or had their research projects curtailed. While still a government employee during the first months of the Eisenhower administration, Carson had been constrained from speaking

President Dwight D. Eisenhower (center) looks on as Douglas McKay (left) is sworn in as his secretary of the interior. McKay branded conservationists "long-haired punks."

out on political issues. Once she became a private citizen, however, she was able to advocate her views publicly.

In a 1953 letter to the *Washington Post*, Carson assailed "the elimination from the government of career men of long experience and high professional competence and their replacement by political appointees." These actions, she went on to charge, "strongly suggest that the way is being cleared for a raid upon our natural resources that is without parallel within the present century." Carson closed her indictment of the Eisenhower administration's approach to conservation with a reference to the government's emphasis on arming itself against the Soviet Union: "It is one of the ironies of our time that, while concentrating on the defense of our country against enemies from without, we should be so heedless of those who would destroy it from within."

Along with her concern about the dismantling of conservation programs, Carson shared in the scientific community's growing uneasiness about nuclear weapons. The nuclear age had been ushered in during World War II, when the United States dropped atomic bombs on the Japanese cities of Hiroshima and Nagasaki in order to hasten the Japanese surrender. Hundreds of thousands of people, virtually all of them civilians, had been killed or wounded by the massive explosions or the deadly radiation released by the blasts. The previously unimaginable destructive capabilities of these weapons gave human beings an unprecedented capacity to destroy one another and poison the environment.

In the aftermath of the August 1945 bombings, the U.S. government had tried to cast nuclear power in a positive light. The Atoms for Peace program offered the hope that nuclear energy could be harnessed for the good of

A lone building stands amid the rubble of Hiroshima. America ushered in the nuclear age when it dropped atomic bombs on two Japanese cities during World War II.

Government scientists use atomic radiation to preserve foods. Carson was skeptical of the claim that nuclear energy was safe for a variety of peacetime applications.

humankind. Government scientists maintained that atomic technology could generate electricity, blast out harbors, propel ships and airplanes, and contribute to the advancement of medicine and scientific knowledge.

In the mid-1950s, however, many leading scientists began to question this optimism. Nobel Prize winner Linus Pauling took the lead in alerting the public to the dangers of nuclear bomb-testing by both the United States and the Soviet Union, and when atomic fallout from these weapons-testing programs was detected across the globe, it was clear that the impact of nuclear weapons could not be re-

stricted to the immediate target area. Most disturbing was the discovery that radioactive substances from nuclear reactions had found their way into the food supply, especially milk. Because these substances were related to a variety of illnesses, including cancer, some scientists insisted that the use of nuclear energy, whether for power plants or weaponry, was dangerous. Rachel Carson read these reports with anxiety. Fully aware that any change in the environment could have unforeseen and far-reaching consequences, she was concerned that the use of a force as tremendous as nuclear power could have a sweeping—and catastrophic—effect on the natural order.

Carson's longtime friend, Olga Owens Huckins, soon told her of another way in which government and industry were tampering with nature. Huckins was an ornithologist (a scientist who studies birds) who wrote articles on nature for a Boston newspaper. Along with her husband, she had established a bird sanctuary at their home in Duxbury, Massachusetts, a small town located between Cape Cod and Boston. Carson regarded Huckins as a keen observer of natural life, a thoughtful woman who did not voice opinions unless she could back them with fact.

In the summer of 1957 the Massachusetts state government had sprayed a pesticide commonly known as DDT over some salt marshes to kill mosquitoes, and the wind had carried the spray over Duxbury and other neighboring towns. The area's mosquitoes were not eradicated; indeed, to a trained observer like Mrs. Huckins, they seemed to have returned as fierce as ever. Worse, she had noted, harmless animals such as birds, grasshoppers, and bees had died wherever the pesticide was sprayed.

Huckins complained to the Massachusetts authorities and was told not to worry: DDT was perfectly safe, they claimed, even when sprayed on humans. She was also informed that because the mosquito population had not been wiped out in the initial spraying, the state was going to repeat the

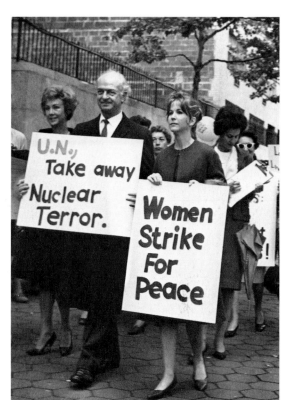

Physicist Linus Pauling joins a rally against nuclear testing. Like Carson, Pauling advocated a cautious approach to technological advancement.

program. Unconvinced by government assurances that DDT was harmless, Huckins researched further and discovered that a similar spraying program on Long Island, New York, had killed fish, birds, and bees in untold numbers. To protest the spraying program, she reported these findings in an angry letter to a Boston newspaper. She then sent a copy of the letter to Carson, along with a request for her assistance in mobilizing the scientific

Carson explores a tidal pool. Because of her love for nature, she felt she could not remain silent about modern technology's threat to the natural order.

support she needed to stop the pesticide spraying.

Carson was well aware of the DDT controversy from her own work with the Fish and Wildlife Service. During World War II, DDT had been so successful in controlling disease-carrying mosquitoes that it was hailed by scientists as the "savior of mankind." After the war, the United States Department of Agriculture (USDA) and other government agencies had conducted tests to determine the safety of DDT for use by farmers and homeowners. The results were controversial. Advocates of the chemical emphasized its usefulness, but other scientists, including Carson's mentor Elmer Higgins, reported that DDT was harmful to wildlife. These scientists wanted to do more research in order to ascertain DDT's long-term effect on humans.

In July 1945 Carson had approached *Reader's Digest* with her ideas for an article on the potential dangers of the pesticide, but the proposal had been rejected. At the time, she was not overly concerned by this rejection be-

Blithely ignoring the pesticide fog surrounding them, children play on swings. Alarm at the pervasive use of such chemicals prompted Carson to write Silent Spring.

cause she believed that the evidence documented by Higgins and others would be heeded and the use of DDT would be strictly regulated. By the time she received Huckins's letter, Carson realized that she had been wrong.

As she began contacting her former colleagues to find out more about the DDT program in Massachusetts and to learn more about the recent research on pesticide use, Carson grew increasingly alarmed. Government researchers continued to document the

hazards of DDT and other powerful new pesticides, but their work was being ignored—or worse, suppressed. In fact, the government had become the chemical pesticide industry's biggest booster. Federal and state officials were not only advocating pesticide use, they were funding massive spraying programs themselves, as they had in Massachusetts. As Carson later commented, "The more I learned about the use of pesticides the more appalled I became. I realized that here was the material for a book. What I discovered was that everything which meant the most to me as a naturalist was being threatened, and that nothing I could do would be more important."

Before she could begin to plan her exposé on chemical pesticides, however, tragedy struck her family. In 1957 her sister Marian's daughter, Marjorie, died. Marjorie was a widow, and her death left her five-year-old son, Roger Christie, without parents. Carson knew that her mother, a 90-year-old in poor health, would be of little help in raising a child. Nevertheless, at age 50 Carson adopted Roger. She raised him just as she had raised his mother almost 20 years earlier.

With a young child in her household, Carson was too busy to take on a major book project. She tried to interest other writers in the pesticide issue, but they insisted that she was the best one to take on the job. After all, she was an established author with scientific credibility, a popular following, and important government contacts. As a compromise, Carson proposed writing a magazine article on the sub-

Carson and her grandnephew, Roger, examine a seashell in 1962. She had adopted the boy five years earlier, following the death of his mother.

ject. But just as it had in 1945, *Reader's Digest*, among other popular magazines, expressed no interest. When *Good Housekeeping* rejected her proposal, the editor informed her that "under no circumstances" would such an article even be considered—it might provoke "unwarranted fear" in readers.

These rejections did not deter Carson—in fact, she came to see them as a challenge. The opposition she encountered to the idea of a book about chemical pesticides convinced her that such a book *had* to be written. More and more she realized, as she wrote a friend, that "there would be no peace for me, if I kept silent."

It had taken her a long time to choose a new book project, and in early 1958 Carson put the reasons for this delay down on paper. She recalled her disquiet about atomic science and the way in which she had repressed her thoughts about this subject; she did not want to believe that the human race could be responsible for so much harm. "It was pleasant to believe," she wrote, "that much of Nature was forever beyond the tampering reach of man: he might level the forests and dam the streams, but the clouds and the rain and the wind were God's. It was comforting to suppose that the stream of life would flow on through time in whatever course God had appointed for it—without interference by one of the drops of that stream, Man. And to suppose that, however the physical environment might mold Life, that Life could never assume the power to change drastically—or even destroy—the physical world."

Carson realized that she could no longer be comforted by such thoughts. As humankind's technological capability grew, so did its capacity for destruction. Unlike many of her colleagues, Carson was ready to confront the truth and acknowledge this fact. "I may not like what I see, but it does no good to ignore it," she wrote. "So it seems time someone wrote of life in the light of the truth as it now appears to us. And I think that may be the book I am to write."

Carson was intrigued by the creatures she glimpsed through her microscope, "living their lives under my lens ... and firing my imagination."

SEVEN

The Truth as She Saw It

In mid-1958 Rachel Carson began researching the book she would later entitle *Silent Spring*. She intended to write a short book that could be published the following year, but it would take her four difficult years to complete the project. The act of writing the book proved to be as difficult and courageous as her decision to tackle so controversial a subject in the first place.

As she worked on the book, Carson was plagued by personal troubles. The first blow came when her mother died in December 1958. The two women had lived together without interruption since the Great Depression. Maria Carson had read and typed her daughter's manuscripts, helped answer her mail, and kept up the household when Carson was working for the government or on a writing project. She had

always been a source of inspiration and encouragement for her daughter's writing and had been especially supportive of her decision to challenge the chemical pesticide industry.

Carson felt this loss keenly. "Her love of life and of all living things was her outstanding quality, of which everybody speaks," Carson wrote of her mother the week of her death. "And while gentle and compassionate, she could fight fiercely against anything she believed wrong, as in our present Crusade! Knowing how she felt about that will help me to return to it soon, and to carry it through to completion."

Carson needed the inspiration that she drew from her mother's memory, for her own health was rapidly deteriorating. "Such a catalogue of illnesses!" she wrote a friend. As she grappled with the research and writing of *Silent*

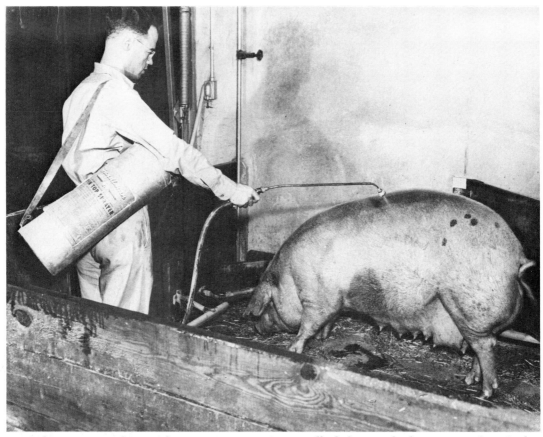

A worker sprays a hog with DDT. Carson was appalled that such dangerous chemicals were infiltrating air, food, and water supplies.

Spring, she suffered from arthritis, sinusitis, bouts of flu, and an ulcer. In 1960 she learned that she had breast cancer—and that the disease was spreading. Weakened and sometimes confined to bed by the radiation treatment she underwent in an attempt to halt the cancer, Carson continued to expand her research, which was yielding evidence far more serious than she, or anyone, had imagined. Indeed, even before her own illness was diagnosed,

she had begun to draw together the scarce but persuasive evidence that exposure to chemical pesticides was a likely cause of some forms of cancer.

The task of collecting and organizing her data on pesticides was overwhelming. In addition to reading hundreds of scientific papers, Carson corresponded with experts from all over the world, including biologists, chemists, agricultural authorities, and medical doctors. Referring to a character from one of

Dead bluefish, mossbunkers, and perch wash up on a New Jersey riverbank. Millions of fish have been killed by pesticides seeping into streams, lakes, and oceans.

New Jersey homes are sprayed with insecticide. Instead of wiping out insect populations, spraying programs sometimes produce pesticide-resistant insects.

Lewis Carroll's fantasy stories, she wrote a friend that "My own work goes on at a furious pace but I feel a little like the Red Queen who had to run as fast as she could just to stay where she was."

Still, as she wrote to her editor in 1959, the tedious process of gathering evidence and checking facts was yielding a book she knew would be important. "Now it is as though all the pieces of an extremely complex jig-saw puzzle are at last falling into place," she wrote. "I have a comforting feeling that what I shall now be able to achieve is a synthesis of widely scattered facts that have not heretofore been considered in relation to each other. It is now possible to build, step-by-step, a really damning case against the use of these chemicals as they are inflicted upon us."

Carson anticipated the furor that the book would provoke and knew that she had to bide her time and build her case carefully. She was well aware that representatives from the pesticide industry and government officials who supported widespread spraying programs would scrutinize *Silent Spring* in an attempt to find misinformation or gaps in her reasoning. Rejecting an invitation by a former colleague to discuss pesticides at an Audubon Society conference, she explained that "the whole thing is so explosive, and the pressures on the other side so powerful and enormous, that I feel it is

wiser to keep my own counsel insofar as I can until I am ready to launch my attack as a whole."

But when Carson learned that plans were underway to spray pesticides near her Maryland home, she became incensed enough to break her own rule and speak out at a community meeting on the proposed spraying. As one of her research assistants later reported, one man called Carson an alarmist. When she calmly began to cite case histories to him, he patronizingly told her that "she really mustn't believe everything she read in the newspapers." Although she had often been characterized as a soft-spoken "nun of nature," Carson fought back with vigor and convinced most of her audience. "She was furious," according to the assistant. "No one, seeing her response that afternoon, could have called her gentle."

But Carson's public appearances were rare during this period; almost all of her time was devoted to completing her book, which was finally finished late in 1961. *Silent Spring* opened with a cautionary tale entitled "A Fable for Tomorrow," which described how people, by their own actions, had brought death to a once beautiful and happy town. "It was a spring without voices," Carson wrote. "On the mornings that had once throbbed with the dawn chorus of robins, catbirds, doves, jays, wrens and scores of other bird voices there was now no sound; only silence lay over the fields and woods and marsh." Carson wrote that in reality no American city had been as decimated by pollution as her ficti-tious town, but she warned that this unthinkable scenario could occur if individuals and governments were not more responsible about using inade-

quately tested chemicals. As Carson pointed out, "This imagined tragedy may easily become a stark reality we all shall know."

Researchers analyze the breeding patterns of corn borers in an attempt to sterilize them. Carson applauded such environmentally sound approaches to pest control.

Carson's basic argument, documented by an appendix that contained more than 50 pages of scientific references, was that advances in modern science had given human beings the capacity to destroy—in just a few years—life forms that had taken eons to evolve. In the past, most living organisms had been able to adjust to gradual changes in the natural environment. But Carson and many of the experts she cited questioned whether animals and plants could adapt to synthetic chemicals that have no equivalent in the natural world.

Given this tremendous power to alter the environment, Carson said, human beings must act with the utmost responsibility, using scientific knowledge intelligently and cautiously. The economic, social, and environmental consequences of new technologies and chemicals must be carefully weighed before they are put into widespread use. The lessons of ecology—the necessity of looking at the "big picture"—must be applied by scientists and governments.

Carson knew that these lessons had not always been heeded, especially with regard to agricultural production. The United States had never seen widespread famine or serious food shortages; indeed, the problem in American agriculture had usually been overproduction—a surplus of agricultural products that lowers farm prices and forces farmers into poverty. Nonetheless, the agricultural industry insisted on the necessity of using increasingly powerful pesticides to maximize crop production.

During World War II a new generation of pesticides came into use, of which DDT was the most widely applied. When some insects became resistant to DDT, more lethal pesticides were invented: aldrin, dieldrin, malathion, and parathion. These powerful pesticides, Carson said, were being used indiscriminately— contaminating plants, soil, animals, and the drinking supply and endangering life everywhere on the planet. She also cited some cases in which pesticide spraying, instead of wiping out insects, had merely created hardy, insecticide-resistant pests.

Carson found convincing evidence that some chemicals become increasingly concentrated, and hence more toxic, as they move up in the food chain. An example she used in *Silent Spring* traced the aftermath of a crop-dusting. After a field of alfalfa is dusted with DDT, alfalfa containing a small amount of DDT residue is fed to cows. Some of the pesticide turns up in the cows' milk, which is in turn consumed by a human being. Because DDT becomes concentrated in fatty sub-

stances, it turns up in an even greater concentration when the milk is churned into butter. Through such a process of transfer, what started out as a very small amount of DDT may end up as a heavy dose in the final product. Because of their place in the food chain, it is human beings who usually consume these final products.

As Carson pointed out in her book, recent pesticide programs had exposed vast geographic areas to a wide array of toxic chemicals. In 1957 and 1958, for example, the USDA attempted to control the fire ant, a South American insect that had been living in the southern United States since the 1920s. The fire ant was a minor nuisance that did not bother humans and did very little economic damage. Yet the USDA decided that the fire ant population should be eradicated and sprayed a solution containing dieldrin (a pesticide 40 times more toxic than DDT) and other chemicals over a 20-million-acre area. Biologists, some of them from the Fish and Wildlife Service, began to report heavy wildlife losses in the sprayed areas. Dehydrated carcasses of quail, wild turkeys, grouse, song birds, opossums, and raccoons were found throughout the area of spraying. Domestic pets and farm animals, including poultry and cows, were affected as well. The pesticides also killed off useful insects that preyed on economically harmful plant-eating pests. As a result, some

Perched on a mountaintop, Carson surveys the countryside. Such excursions were rare in the 1960s, as illness and professional demands kept her at home much of the time.

The sores on this seal's back were caused by water pollution. In Silent Spring, *Carson urged her readers to consider the unwanted side effects of technological progress.*

farm areas exposed to the chemicals suffered an infestation of sugarcane borers (insects that feed on sugarcane) that did great damage to the sugarcane crop.

The USDA denied that the pesticide spraying was responsible for these catastrophes, but the Food and Drug Administration (FDA), responding to the protests of farmers, outdoor enthusiasts, and conservationists, ultimately ordered a stop to the pesticide program. Fire ants continued to thrive, though no one was seriously bothered. The only group that had gained from the sprayings, according to a trade

journal quoted by Carson, was the pesticide manufacturers who "tapped a sales bonanza."

Carson was not opposed to controlling insect pests when necessary, but the safer way, she proposed, was to use the systems of nature itself. To control crop-eating insects, farmers could use ladybugs, praying mantises, and other "beneficial" insects that fed on pests. Scientists had also developed methods of preventing harmful insects from reproducing; in addition, bacterial agents and viral strains, safe for humans, had been successful in controlling targeted pests. For example, a powdery bacterium called milky spore had succeeded in controlling Japanese beetle infestations where more expensive and dangerous pesticide programs had failed. Because they were part of the natural order, Carson advocated these and other biological solutions to the problems of pest control. She pointed out that these approaches are "based on understanding of the living organisms they seek to control, and of the whole fabric of life to which organisms belong."

Perhaps the most controversial sections of *Silent Spring* were the chapters dealing with the effect of chemical pesticides on human genetics and public health. Carson was very cautious here, noting that not enough research had been done to draw definitive conclusions. But there was, she insisted, sufficient evidence to suspect that exposure to chemical pesticides caused stillbirths and genetic deformities as well as certain cancers and other diseases.

Scientists now know a good deal more about genetic theory and the causes of disease than they did when Carson was writing her book. New research has shown that her concern about public health was on the mark. The origins of genetic damage, cancer, and other serious diseases are complex, but the chemical pollution of the human environment is certainly a contributing factor.

Silent Spring presented its readers with a simple but critical choice. "We stand now where two roads diverge," Carson wrote in the book's closing chapter. She described "the road we have long been traveling"—the use of inadequately tested chemicals—as being "deceptively easy, a smooth superhighway on which we progress with great speed, but at its end lies disaster." Quoting poet Robert Frost's "The Road Not Taken," Carson pointed out that the careful, ecologically sound path was humankind's only other option. "The other fork of the road—the one 'less traveled by'—offers our last, our only chance to reach a destination that assures the preservation of the earth."

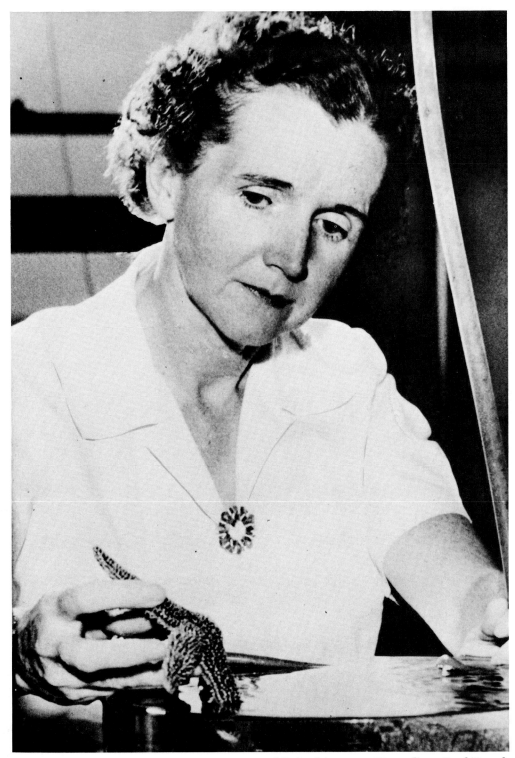

Carson's masterpiece, Silent Spring, *was published in 1962. Her editor Paul Brooks marveled that "she succeeded in making a book about death a celebration of life."*

EIGHT

A Legacy of Life

The launching of *Silent Spring* took place on June 16, 1962, when the first part of a serialized, condensed version of the book appeared in the *New Yorker*. Although Carson had hoped her indictment of inadequately tested pesticides would touch a chord in her readers, she was nonetheless startled by the widespread public support she received. Admiring letters and telegrams poured in to the magazine. Praise and concern from ordinary citizens and prominent scientists reached as far as the White House. President John F. Kennedy acknowledged that the furor over Carson's series in the *New Yorker* had prodded his administration to reevaluate federal pesticide regulations.

But Carson's work drew as much criticism as praise—and her detractors were even more vocal than her supporters. A headline in the *New York Times* summed up the controversy: "SILENT SPRING IS NOW NOISY SUMMER." Led by chemical company representatives, the attack was vicious and emotional. Because Carson's careful research had left her virtually unassailable from a factual standpoint, many of her opponents launched campaigns to discredit her personally. A member of a government board on pest control even ridiculed Carson's marital status. "I thought she was a spinster," he remarked. "What's she so worried about genetics for?"

The *New Yorker* serialization prompted the Velsicol Chemical Corporation to send Carson's publisher a five-page letter recommending that the company abandon its plans to publish *Silent Spring* in book form. Implying that the work was part of a communist

President John F. Kennedy feeds deer in a national park. Impressed by Silent Spring, *Kennedy ordered a reevaluation of federal pesticide policy.*

lent Spring as scheduled on September 27, 1962. As the book rose to the top of the best-seller list, the advocates of chemical pesticide use stepped up their counterattack. The National Agricultural Chemicals Association budgeted a quarter of a million dollars to distribute a booklet attacking Carson's facts. The American Medical Association, the agribusiness (large farming) industry, and a number of publications that received revenue from chemical industry advertisements all criticized Carson's book.

Her opponents often resorted to satire and parody to distort her arguments. One well-known chemical company printed a mock version of *Silent Spring* entitled "The Desolate Year." Misstating Carson's position that chemical pesticides ought to be studied and regulated, not banned, the parody described a barren, insect-ravaged world in which pesticides had been prohibited. Typical of the attacks on Carson, the pamphlet insinuated that Carson was concerned about protecting insects, not human life.

Despite these distortions, the message of *Silent Spring* was heeded by millions—including officials in the Kennedy administration. The President's Science Advisory Committee (PSAC) launched an eight-month investigation into the dangers and benefits of pesticide use. Carson, along with government officials and representatives of the chemical industry, testified

plot to undermine the economies of Western nations, the letter referred to "sinister influences, whose attacks on the chemical industry have a dual purpose: (1) to create the false impression that all business is grasping and immoral, and (2) to reduce the use of agricultural chemicals in this country and in the countries of western Europe, so that our supply of food will be reduced to east-curtain parity."

But despite these and other protests, Houghton Mifflin published *Si-*

This British cartoon attests to the worldwide impact of Carson's book. Silent Spring *incited controversy and sparked legislation across the globe.*

Rachel Carson died on April 14, 1964. Her love of nature lives on in projects such as this Maine wildlife refuge, which bears her name.

before the panel. The PSAC's final report echoed many of the positions in *Silent Spring*: It called for greater government involvement in monitoring and controlling pesticide use, criticized misguided "eradication" programs such as the drive to wipe out the fire ant, and decried the government's lax attitude on human safety. On May 15, 1963, the day the report was issued, a headline in the *Christian Science Monitor* proclaimed "RACHEL CARSON STANDS VINDICATED."

The PSAC's endorsement, coupled with Carson's appearance on the CBS television program "The Silent Spring of Rachel Carson" a few months earlier, began to turn the tide of public opinion. Influential publications that had printed attacks on *Silent Spring*, such as *Science* magazine and *Reader's Digest*, began to reconsider their judgments. The popular newsweekly *Time*, which in 1962 condemned Carson's book as an "emotional and inaccurate outburst," reversed its position.

More important, the public began to rally to the environmentalist cause. Conservation organizations grew in size and in political importance. Politicians who once ignored the environmental issue now wrote to Carson asking for her advice. By the end of 1962, more than 40 pesticide-regulating bills had been introduced in state legislatures across the nation. The most sweeping change came in 1964, when Congress amended federal law to shift the burden of proof in safety debates. Government agencies no longer had to prove that specific chemical formulations were hazardous; now it was up to manufacturers to demonstrate the safety of their products *before* they could be marketed. *Silent Spring* was translated into more than a dozen foreign languages and sparked worldwide discussion about the dangers of pesticides. Several countries passed new laws regulating the chemical industry. Referring to a highly toxic group of pesticides criticized in *Silent Spring*, a British politician tried to sway the vote on pending legislation with a joke about a cannibal chief "who now no longer allows his tribe to eat Americans because their fat is contaminated with chlorinated hydrocarbons."

As her ideas gained acceptance, the author of *Silent Spring* was showered with awards and honors. At her induction into the American Academy of Arts and Letters, whose 50 members included the most respected artists, writers, and musicians in the country, she was lauded as "a scientist in the grand literary style [who] has used her scientific knowledge and moral feeling

This commemorative stamp was issued in 1981 as part of the U.S. Postal Service's "Great Americans" series.

to deepen our consciousness of living nature." The National Wildlife Federation, the Garden Club of America, the American Geographical Society, and the Animal Welfare Institute were among other organizations that honored her. Carson often used these ceremonial occasions to rally support for environmentalism. When she became the first woman to be awarded the Audubon Medal, she warned that the battle was far from over. "Conservation is a cause that has no end. There is no point at which we will say 'our work is finished.'"

But Carson's failing health sometimes made it difficult for her to make public appearances. Her cancer continued to spread, and perhaps the controversy over *Silent Spring* further sapped her strength. Yet she persisted in her campaign against the irresponsible use of chemicals, sacrificing her health and comfort because she knew that she had the ear of the public and felt it was essential that she continue to speak out. Carson was even able to joke about her situation. In 1963 she wrote a friend: "I have now reached that state of eminence where my sniffles, like the President's, are news. The morning paper explains my failure to appear at the Air Pollution Conference with a fairly conspicuous article carrying the heading, 'Author of *Silent Spring* Silenced by Cold.' What good news in chemical circles!"

Carson retained her love of nature to the end. Accompanied by her 11-year-old adopted son and two cats, she made her last visit to her summer home in Maine in 1963. Too ill to scramble on the rocks along the tidal shore or go bird watching in the nearby woods, she nonetheless remained a keen observer of nature. She could no longer collect samples herself, but she still enjoyed studying the tiny denizens of the tide pools under

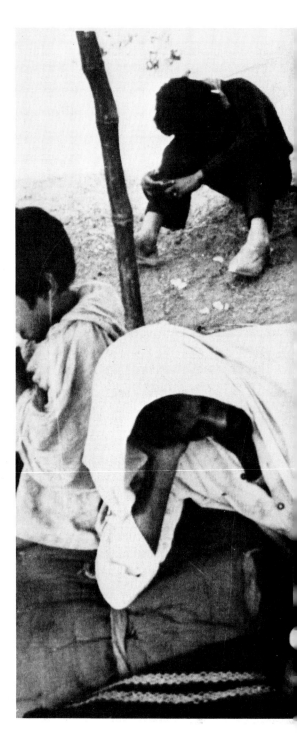

Residents of Bhopal, India, suffer the effects of a 1984 leak at a pesticide factory. The tragedy killed thousands, a reminder that the dangers Carson warned about still exist.

her microscope. And although she was virtually confined to a wheelchair, early that fall Carson traveled to California, where she visited a redwood forest, realizing a longtime dream.

Rachel Carson died at her Maryland home on April 14, 1964, at the age of 56. Conservationists, politicians, and scientists joined her friends and family at the funeral, held a few days later. Great Britain's Prince Philip sent a large wreath, and her pallbearers included Senator Abraham Ribicoff and Secretary of the Interior Stewart Udall.

During her memorial service, one of Carson's admirers read a letter Carson had written a friend after a morning spent watching monarch butterflies. The insects were preparing to migrate south for what she called "the closing journey of their lives." Carson, who knew that she, too, was nearing the end, reminded her friend that "it had been a happy spectacle, that we had felt no sadness when we spoke of the fact that there would be no return." The letter continued:

> And rightly—for when any living thing has come to the end of its cycle we accept that end as natural. For the Monarch butterfly, that cycle is measured in a known span of months. For ourselves, the measure is something else, the span of which we cannot know. But the thought is the same: when that intangible cycle has run its course it is a natural and not unhappy thing that a life comes to its end. That is what those brightly fluttering bits of life taught me this morning.

In the years since her death, Carson's memory has been honored in numerous ways. A Rachel Carson National Wildlife Refuge was set up near her summer home in Maine. The federal government issued a postage stamp with her picture on it. In 1980 Jimmy Carter awarded her a Presidential Medal of Freedom posthumously, the highest civilian honor awarded by the U.S. government. On the certificate that accompanied the award, the president called Carson "A biologist with a gentle, clear voice" who "warned Americans of the dangers human beings themselves pose for their own environment."

The greatest aspect of Carson's extraordinary legacy remains her books, which reveal her gift for language, her love of knowledge, and her profound concern for the fate of the earth. Today she is best remembered for *Silent Spring*, her eloquent warning about humankind's capacity to destroy the natural order, but her other books, which celebrate the intricate web of life, were her personal favorites. Shortly before her death, Carson wrote, "It is good to know that I shall live on even in the minds of many who do not know me and largely through association with things that are beautiful and lovely."

In order to protect the complex network of life that she studied, wrote about, and loved, Carson took on the onerous task of exposing the human

St. Louis students protest air pollution as part of 1970's Earth Day. The ecological principles espoused by Carson have gained acceptance around the world.

Nuclear power is even more controversial now than in Carson's day. Scientists still cannot answer many questions about radiation containment and atomic waste disposal.

race's capacity for destruction. She had no illusions that the battle against environmental pollution would be easily won. Indeed, the arrogance toward nature that frightened Carson and inspired her to write *Silent Spring* is still very much in evidence.

Irresponsible segments of the chemical industry, though chastened by her book, were not defeated. DDT and other dangerous pesticides were banned in the United States and other Western countries, but some pesticide manufacturers found new markets in the developing nations known as the Third

World, where regulations were lax. Environmental disasters have occurred with alarming frequency; and, as if to underline Carson's belief in the interconnectedness of planetary life, no part of the world has been exempt. Residents of Love Canal, New York, were forced to abandon their homes because nearby areas were used as a chemical dump. The 2,500 residents of Times Beach, a small agricultural community in Missouri, likewise had to abandon their homes and relocate because dioxin, the poisonous by-product of a chemical pesticide, had contaminated the soil. In Seveso, Italy, an accident at a pesticide plant released this same chemical; 700 people had to be evacuated and crops were destroyed within a five-mile radius of the factory. In Bhopal, India, a gas used in the manufacture of pesticides escaped into the atmosphere, causing thousands of deaths. The cautionary "Fable for Tomorrow" with which Carson opened *Silent Spring* does not seem as alarmist as it did in the 1960s.

Yet significant gains have been made in the years since the book's publication. The environmentalist movement grew throughout the 1960s, and scores of state and federal laws reflecting this trend were passed. In 1970 millions of people throughout the world celebrated the first "Earth Day," a day for individuals to affirm their commitment to the ecological principles that Carson popularized. That same year, the fed-

President Jimmy Carter said of Rachel Carson in 1980: "Always concerned, always eloquent, she created a tide of environmental consciousness that has not ebbed."

eral government responded to growing political pressure by creating the Environmental Protection Agency to coordinate and enforce regulations safeguarding America's air, water, and land. Carson did not live to see these developments, but they are part of her legacy.

Before Carson wrote *Silent Spring*, few people comprehended the noxious effects that pollution could have on public health and the natural world. Few understood the ecological principle that all life is interrelated. Because of Rachel Carson's courage, determination, and eloquence, these ideas have become widespread. Millions of people all over the globe have begun to take responsibility for the natural environment, and because of this commitment, they are willing to stand and be counted in the battle to protect life on earth. They are men and women who accept Carson's pronouncement that given humankind's newfound capacity to control—and destroy—the natural order, the human race now faces the challenge of proving "our maturity and our mastery, not of nature, but of ourselves."

FURTHER READING

Brooks, Paul. *The House of Life: Rachel Carson at Work.* New York: Fawcett Books, 1974.

———. *Speaking for Nature: How Literary Naturalists from Henry Thoreau to Rachel Carson Have Shaped America.* Boston: Houghton Mifflin, 1980.

Carson, Rachel. *The Edge of the Sea.* Boston: Houghton Mifflin, 1955.

———. *The Sea Around Us.* New York: Oxford University Press, 1961.

———. *The Sense of Wonder.* New York: Harper & Row, 1965.

———. *Silent Spring.* Boston: Houghton Mifflin, 1962.

———. *Under the Sea-Wind: A Naturalist's Picture of Ocean Life.* New York: Oxford University Press, 1952.

Gartner, Carol B. *Rachel Carson.* New York: Ungar, 1985.

Graham, Frank, Jr. *Since Silent Spring.* New York: Fawcett Books, 1977.

Sterling, Philip. *Sea and Earth: The Life of Rachel Carson.* New York: Crowell, 1970.

CHRONOLOGY

May 27, 1907	Rachel Carson born in Springdale, Pennsylvania
1925–29	Attends the Pennsylvania College for Women
1929	Spends summer at Woods Hole Marine Biological Laboratory on Cape Cod
1929–32	Studies at Johns Hopkins University; graduates with an M.A. in marine zoology
1935	Begins writing radio scripts for United States Bureau of Fisheries
1936	Becomes junior aquatic biologist with Bureau of Fisheries
	Carson's sister dies; her two teenage daughters join the Carson household
1937	Carson's article "Undersea" is published in the *Atlantic Monthly*
1941	Carson publishes first book, *Under the Sea-Wind*
	United States enters World War II
1942	Carson becomes assistant to the chief of the office of information at U.S. Fish and Wildlife Service
1949	Named editor-in-chief for all Fish and Wildlife publications
1951	Publishes *The Sea Around Us*
1952	*Under the Sea-Wind* is republished, joins *The Sea Around Us* on the best-seller list
	Carson ends her civil service career to become a full-time writer
1955	*The Edge of the Sea* is published
1956	"Help Your Child to Wonder" (later published in book form as *The Sense of Wonder*) appears in *Woman's Home Companion*
1957	Carson's niece Marjorie dies; Carson adopts her son Roger
1960	Begins cancer treatment
1962	*Silent Spring* is published
1963	The President's Science Advisory Committee endorses Carson's ideas in its report on pesticide use
April 14, 1964	Carson dies of cancer

INDEX

INDEX

PICTURE CREDITS

Marty Jezer is the author of *The Dark Ages: Life in the United States, 1945 to 1960* and numerous articles and essays about American history, culture, and life. He lives in Vermont with his wife and daughter.

❖   ❖   ❖

Matina S. Horner is president of Radcliffe College and associate professor of psychology and social relations at Harvard University. She is best known for her studies of women's motivation, achievement, and personality development. Dr. Horner serves on several national boards and advisory councils, including those of the National Science Foundation, Time Inc., and the Women's Research and Education Institute. She earned her B. A. from Bryn Mawr College and Ph.D. from the University of Michigan, and holds honorary degrees from many colleges and universities, including Mount Holyoke, Smith, Tufts, and the University of Pennsylvania.